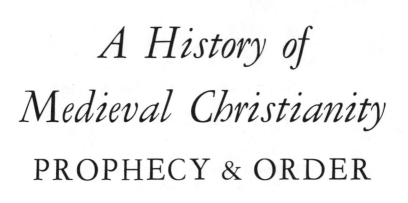

A History of
Medieval Christianity
PROPHECY & ORDER

OTHER BOOKS BY *Jeffrey Burton Russell*

Dissent and Reform in the Early Middle Ages   1965
Medieval Civilization   1968
Witchcraft in the Middle Ages   1972
The Devil: Perceptions of Evil from Antiquity
to Primitive Christianity   1977

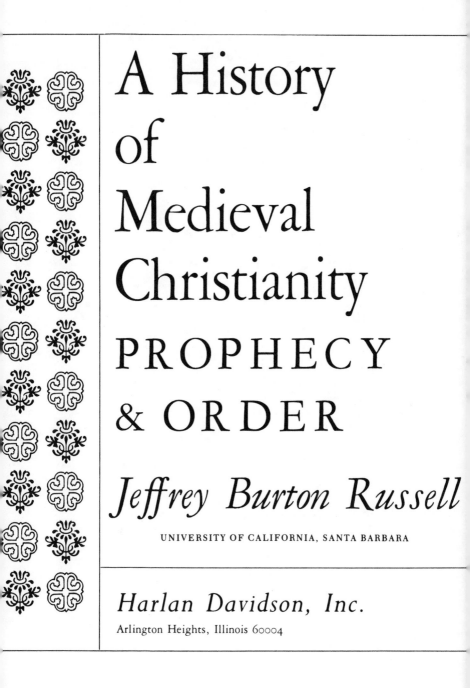

A History of Medieval Christianity

PROPHECY & ORDER

Jeffrey Burton Russell

UNIVERSITY OF CALIFORNIA, SANTA BARBARA

Harlan Davidson, Inc.

Arlington Heights, Illinois 60004

For Jennifer

Library of Congress Cataloging-in-Publication Data

Russell, Jeffrey Burton.
A history of medieval Christianity.

Reprint. Originally published: New York: Crowell,
1968.
Bibliography: p.
Includes index.
1. Church history—Middle Ages, 600–1500. 2. Europe
—Church history—Middle Ages, 600–1500. I. Title.
BR252.R8   1986   270   86-9014
ISBN 0-88295-761-9

MANUFACTURED IN THE UNITED STATES OF AMERICA
90 89   CM   14 15 16

Preface

The history of medieval Christianity can be approached in a number of ways, among which none is more significant than to investigate the tension within the Church between the spirit of prophecy and the spirit of order. Both spirits are in the tradition of Jesus, and both are progressive. Both are opposed to the self-satisfied defense of the status quo that has too often characterized Christianity since the end of the great persecutions. Both seek to lead men into the imitation of Christ. But the spirit of order has attempted to reform men and their institutions to correspond with the will of God, while the spirit of prophecy has sought to *transform* them, to lift them out of this world into the world and life of God.

I have in this book attempted to show both the importance of these two forces taken separately and the creativity of their opposition. Yet I have not attempted to prove the unprovable—that this tension is the only important dynamic in Christian history. This book is not a monograph and certainly not a polemic. It is a general history of medieval Christianity that emphasizes one of its fundamental conflicts.

I wish to express my appreciation to the Research Committee of the University of California, Riverside, for its support of clerical expenses; and I want to thank the editorial staff of the College Department of the Thomas Y. Crowell Company for their effort and their pleasant cooperation. Many thanks to my wife, Diana, who must hate the very sight of a galley proof but who would never say so.

J.B.R.

v

Contents

Prophecy and Order

The Christian spirit has always been ambivalent toward this world. On the one hand, the spirit of prophecy, rooted in the tradition of Isaiah and Jeremiah, has insisted that this world, its men and its institutions, are under judgment. Our duty, it says, is to strive for a radical transformation of the world in order to destroy the obstacles erected by society between ourselves and the transcendent God. On the other hand, the spirit of order has called for a progressive, creative, and often very moderate program of reshaping this world and its institutions on the model of God's world. Both prophecy and order seek the Kingdom of God; but prophecy seeks the end of the world and uncompromisingly hopes for immediate confrontation with God, while order works more patiently within the world and with the imperfect materials at hand.

In medieval Christianity, as in Christianity as a whole, both the prophetic spirit and the spirit of order were at work, sometimes in cooperation and sometimes in conflict. There are other ways of viewing the medieval Church; but as history is not a bare account of "what happened," but an investigation of what happened with the intent of discerning significant patterns, the study of the Church in terms of the complementary forces of prophecy and order is legitimate.

1

Medieval Christianity, then, is an integral part of medieval society, affecting as well as affected by the other human institutions and ideas surrounding it. The study of medieval Christianity both illuminates and is illuminated by medieval history as a whole.

But equally important, the medieval is one phase, and chronologically the longest phase, in the history of Christianity itself. For at least a century now, all reputable scholars of whatever faith have accepted the notion of development in the history of the Church. Old-fashioned Catholics liked to believe that the Catholic Church of the nineteenth century was in essentials identical with the Church of the first century; old-fashioned Protestants insisted that only what was explicitly biblical was true Christianity. All now recognize that in the beginning the apostles had only a very disorganized and inchoate set of ideas about Christ and that all the elaborations of Christian theology, ethics, anthropology, and sociology had gradually and painstakingly to be worked out in the course of centuries. The historian, whose raison d'être is to study change in society, is primarily concerned in his study of the Church with this process of development.

The history of Christianity is far more than the history of the Church as an institution. It is the study of the life of the Christian people (of the Church in its broadest sense), their ideas, their ways, their feelings, without undue scrupulosity or concern for formal institutional definitions. When seen in this proper historical perspective, the Church is not a well-designed architectural construction—let alone the monolith that the ill-informed suppose it to be—but a diverse structure housing artifacts of varying designs, some large, some small, some beautiful, some ugly. The historian recognizes that to describe the development of such complex patterns is inevitably to do them violence, and if he does not therefore shirk the task, it is only with the wholesome understanding that no problem is ever really done justice by the human mind.

Being human, and studying humans, the historian is not content simply to describe the dynamics and mechanics of the development of medieval Christianity. It is true that he is not concerned with "the descent of the Dove" as the English novelist and historian

2

Charles Williams put it: the action of the Holy Spirit within the Church. Whether or not he is a believer, the historian has no access, at least as an historian, to the mind of God, and he does not presume to interpret that mind to his audience. He is obliged by the limitations of his knowledge and of his method to examine religions and religious institutions as the products of human enterprise, reserving his judgment of their metaphysical implications for such times as he acts, not as an historian, but as a speculative philosopher. But the historian does judge (without denominational prejudice) whether or not the development of the medieval Church was a true expression of religion, a true expression of the pristine Christian spirit.

A German Protestant historian, Rudolf Sohm, once accused the Church of transforming itself from a sacrament to a corporation; Will Herberg, the sociologist and theologian, has warned that religion must never put the stamp of approval upon any given system of society. Was the medieval Church guilty of answering the demands of society too well? Did it, in its desire for order, too often validate the cultures in which it dwelt, forgetting the demands of prophecy that culture be brought to judgment? As was remarked recently of the present, "Religion is a life decision, not something infused along with American citizenship. It is a commitment of life, not a mouthful of slogans."[1] The religion that complacently defends all the values of the surrounding society has ceased to be religion and has instead become false religiosity. Miguel de Unamuno, who called himself a Catholic heretic, thus indicted the search for a Christian order: " 'Christianity' has come to serve as designation for the Christian quality of a supposed community of Christians, a Christian society. But this is obviously an absurdity, since society kills Christianity, which is always an affair of solitary individuals...."[2]

There were many varieties of religious expression in the Middle Ages. But was medieval Christianity as a whole conducive to a

[1]Bruce Vawter, "The Beast from the Sea," *Commonweal*, LXXX (May 22, 1964), 255.

[2]*The Agony of Christianity* (New York, 1960), p. 24.

valid expression of the religious experience? It would be uncommonly presumptuous to claim to know for certain what constitutes true religious experience, and the historian shuns judgments based upon orthodoxies established by any denomination or upon the whims of his personal conscience. But philosophers of religion (to name only a few from different generations, William James, Rudolf Otto, and Mircea Eliade) have given us something to work with. Some degree of support would be obtained for the statement that the religious experience is the immediate and personal sense of the holy: the always inexplicable, incomprehensible, and often terrifying majesty and mystery of the "Wholly Other" who is nevertheless here now and always everywhere. The attitudes that proceed from a generalization of this experience constitute a *sacred view of the world*. In the sacred view of the world, nothing is profane but all things are sacred; in the profane view, presently far more common, nothing is sacred but all things are profane. Wordsworth, oppressed by the rise of the profane view of the universe, complained:

> *The world is too much with us; late and soon,*
> *Getting and spending, we lay waste our powers;*
> *Little we see in nature that is ours;*
> *We have given our hearts away, a sordid boon!*
> *This Sea that bares her bosom to the moon,*
> *The winds that will be howling at all hours,*
> *And are up-gathered now like sleeping flowers,*
> *For this, for everything, we are out of tune;*
> *It moves us not.—Great God! I'd rather be*
> *A Pagan suckled in a creed outworn;*
> *So might I, standing on this pleasant lea,*
> *Have glimpses that would make me less forlorn;*
> *Have sight of Proteus rising from the sea;*
> *Or hear old Triton blow his wreathèd horn.*

The sense of the sacred is that everything in the universe is either God (pantheism or emanationism) or filled with God like a sponge immersed in the sea (immanentism). This sense is at the base of all religions; but it tends to fade somewhat as they become institutionalized. The ecstasies of the early Orphic religion in Greece, for example, contrast with the publicly ordained and publicly performed worship of the staid and not wholly compelling Olympic pantheon of classical times. In the search for order, the prophetic spirit is often denied. The tradition of the Christian Church has been to straddle the sacred and the profane and persistently to maintain that some things are holy, like churches, and others profane, like marketplaces. It is against this dichotomy that many current theologians are striving, either to restore to the churches the immediate sense of the otherness of God or else to convince them of the infinite worth of the "secular city" they had scorned as profane.

Did the medieval Church, then, encourage a true religious sense? In one sense, Sohm is right: the Church did turn itself into a corporation. It did become involved in the pursuit of wealth, status, and political power. It did invest much time and energy in the construction and the maintenance of its own hierarchical structure. St. Bernard once observed with prophetic dismay that the pope spent not every day, but every hour of the day in administrative matters. St. Peter has always been the type of the Church, cowardly, stupid, and indecisive. Yet in the end Peter proved faithful and brave. The Church was necessarily a failure in that its organizational structure muffled the immediacy of the religious experience. Its search for *order* frustrated *prophecy*. Yet this search was also completely necessary. Christianity can get along neither within the Church nor without it. The demise of Gnosticism, which had no lasting ecclesiastical organization, is evidence that without a structure and a system of authority, no body of doctrines can long endure: either it will undergo such strange metamorphoses as to make it unrecognizably different from its origins, or else it will simply perish. It was the necessary work of the Church, and a work in which it was quite successful, both to keep the doctrines of Christ alive and to keep its development of his teachings within the boundaries of a recognizable tradition.

Like Peter, the Church is necessarily a failure, yet absolutely necessary. The search for order and the urge to prophecy, the progressives who make necessary adjustments and the conservatives who check the tendency to proceed too far or too fast, the constitutional structure of the Church and the mystics and ascetics who cried down or ignored the structure, the orthodox and the heretics—all these opposites are necessary. Christianity was able to preserve its doctrinal and institutional identity while at the same time producing (or at least permitting) a wealth and variety of religious experience unparalleled in the history of other religions. It was able to do this through the salutary and never-resolved tension between prophecy and order.

It is indisputable that, regardless of the need for order in the development of society and institutions, the founder of Christianity was a prophet. Christ taught the uprooting and reversal of most of the values that characterized society in his day. He did not, as some of his more extreme followers maintained, teach that the world was unreal or that it was evil, but neither did he come, as many of the Jews supposed, to build a kingdom of this world. Christ vehemently rejected the status quo. He insisted that his mission was a complete transformation of the world as we know it.

To go much beyond this in describing the career of Jesus in a book of this kind would be unfair to a subject that perplexes scholars and believers alike and has produced a literature that exceeds both in volume and in complexity that on any other problem. Yet since it is impossible to understand medieval Christianity without some reference to its backgrounds, it is necessary to raise, while not presuming to answer, some of the outstanding questions.

The problem of the historical Jesus is enormously complex. In his own time, the Romans thought him a fanatic, many of the Jews despised him as a charlatan or hated him as a blasphemer, and even his friends at times wondered whether he were not mad (Mark 3:21). But shortly after his death and resurrection, a community called Christians existed who accepted none of these explanations but rather that of Peter. "Who say you that I am?" Peter was asked, and he replied, "Thou art the Christ, the Son of the living God." And Jesus said, "Flesh and blood have not revealed this to you, Simon son of Jonah, but my Father who is in heaven" (Matthew 16:16–17). This was accepted absolutely uncritically by Christians until well into the eighteenth century and it was rejected by non-Christians equally uncritically. Until the eighteenth century, the techniques and philosophy of historical investigation and textual criticism had not yet been developed to a level permitting a critical, analytical historical approach to the personality of Jesus. From the time of Hermann Reimarus[3] to that of Albert Schweitzer,[4] historians of all varieties tried to answer the question, What really *was* the personality of Jesus? The quest led them into areas shunned by previous Christians as untouchable. Catholics had argued that their church was essentially the same as that of the apostles; Protestants had argued that it was necessary to return to the pristine religion of the Bible. But modern historians and critics questioned the reliability of both the apostles and the Bible.

The attempt to approach the Bible and the personality of Jesus historically in much the same way as one approaches the *Commentaries on the Gallic Wars* and the personality of Caesar is from a scholarly standpoint unimpeachable. There is no area of either natural or human history that human reason should not freely investigate to the limits of its ability. But the historians underestimated the difficulty of their material. Problems of biblical criticism have grown more and more complex, and new questions have been raised more frequently than old ones answered. Furthermore, the personality of Jesus, unlike that of Caesar, is one that has had a deep meaning for people in every generation, so that each generation tends to interpret him to fit its needs. The

[3]*Von dem Zwecke Jesu und Seiner Jünger* (1778).
[4]*The Quest of the Historical Jesus* (London, 1906).

7

historians of the Enlightenment tried to rationalize away the miracles; some late-nineteenth-century historians, carried away by the emerging science of anthropology and mythology, declared that Jesus was only a myth; progressive liberals at the turn of the century made him a social worker and teacher; a businessman of the 1920's painted him as the most successful salesman of all time. In the twentieth century one of the strongest schools, championed originally by Rudolf Bultmann (who has, like all good scholars, modified his views with time), has declared Jesus to be an eschatological prophet: one who predicted the imminent end of the world and its transformation into the Kingdom of God. The duty of the individual Christian is, then, to face the ultimate reality he is about to encounter. This eschatological interpretation has many merits, and its defenders, particularly Bultmann, have bolstered it by a rigorous textual analysis of the Scriptures known as "form criticism." Yet the present popularity of the interpretation seems due at least partly to the readiness with which it can be incorporated into existentialist philosophies urging the necessity of the individual's facing reality in each present moment.

Schweitzer and many other twentieth-century theologians have argued from these changes in fashion that the historical search for the personality of Jesus is futile and that therefore each individual in every generation must in fact interpret him for himself. Bultmann said, for example, that though the Resurrection could not be accepted as an historical fact, it remained, and justly so, the center of the individual's experience of Christianity. Lately such views, which were on their way to becoming standard, have been cogently questioned. James Robinson[5] points out that the earlier historians had asked too much. They had assumed, as good nineteenth-century positivists, that history could tell them "how it really happened," and when they found that it could not, they either gave up or retreated into solipsism. But historians today do not believe that history can say fully how any event "really happened," because they know that the matter of history is far too

[5]*The New Quest of the Historical Jesus* (London, 1959).

complex, and that the human mind is far too limited, ever to construct a truly objective history. What historians do today is use the evidence they have to create a coherent, consistent picture of how individuals *appeared* to themselves and to others. In this new approach, while the problem of Jesus remains extremely difficult, it is in the same category as the problem of Caesar, say, or of Franklin D. Roosevelt.

Though we shall never know *exactly* what Jesus—or Roosevelt—was or thought, each new investigation and interpretation brings us a bit closer, so that at least we can say what he was not. He was much more a prophet than a liberal reformer.

Primitive Christianity

Christianity was established by Christ, but it was established in a particular social and intellectual context; and its origins are to be sought not only in the personality of Jesus, but in the first-century milieu.

Jesus and his immediate followers were all Jews, and the strongest influences upon Christianity derive either from traditional or from Essenic Judaism. Many of the teachings of Jesus are rooted in orthodox Jewish tradition: his strict monotheism, for example; his reverence for the Scriptures; and his attention to Jewish festivals and the Jewish law. Many of the ethical teachings of Christ resemble very closely those of the great rabbis of his time and of the preceding century. For example, his insistence that the law is made for man and not the other way round and that it therefore must be modified when mercy and justice demand, closely parallels the thought of the great Rabbi Hillel. It is clear that the writers of the Gospels, particularly Matthew, took care to show how the events of Christ's life and death fulfilled the prophecies of the Old Testament. Many of the Jews supposed that Jesus was come as the Messiah and received him into Jerusalem with joy on Palm Sunday, only to be subsequently disappointed when he refused to lead them in an uprising against the Romans. But there was another messianic tradition that Jesus' followers claimed he did fulfill: that of the "suffering servant" (Isaiah 53) who lays down his life for the people. Behind this tradition were two ancient Jewish customs, that of the scapegoat, an animal upon whom all the sins of the community were ceremonially placed and who then was driven out and killed, and that of the *go'el,* a relative responsible for the actions and the welfare of each family.

Christianity was also related to the Essene tradition. The Essenes were an ascetic group who drew apart from the rest of the Jews and settled along the desolate shores of the Dead Sea. Enough has long been known of them so that it was possible for Frederick the Great of Prussia to write to D'Alembert in 1770 that Jesus might have been an Essene. Then, in 1947, when a Bedouin shepherd boy accidentally discovered an ancient storage jar full of scrolls in a cave near the Dead Sea, began a series of archeological finds of the utmost importance. One has only to look at the sheer volume of literature on the Dead Sea Scrolls, both scholarly and popular, that the presses have poured out since 1950 to recognize the effects of this momentous discovery. By now (1968), a dozen caves have been discovered containing countless scrolls and documents. The general scholarly consensus is that these documents were cached there by the Essenic community of Qumran, which was destroyed in the year 70 in the general overthrow and diaspora of the Jewish nation by the Roman armies following an unsuccessful uprising.

Qumran was founded somewhere around 175 B.C. and thus was flourishing at the time of Jesus. In the first flush of excitement following the discovery of the scrolls, a number of writers incautiously leaped to unjustified conclusions and claimed to have found in the Essenic reference to a "Teacher of Righteousness," persecuted by evil priests and done to death by the people, the perfect prototype of Jesus. Those who, like Edmund Wilson, sought a stick with which to beat Christianity asserted that here was the proof that Jesus was merely imitating an earlier prophet.

11

Better translations and more careful study have shown that the Teacher of Righteousness was not really killed by the people and that he was a political opponent of the Maccabees bearing little resemblance to Jesus. Yet there are many ways in which Essenism and Christianity do resemble each other closely. Asceticism, distrust of and withdrawal from the world, rejection of accepted morality for a higher purity, are common to both. More striking is the imagery and language they share. The Epistles of St. Paul, and more particularly the Gospel according to St. John, show close ties with the Essene spirit. In St. John, the world is created by the Word of God, as for the Essenes it is created by his Wisdom. The imagery of opposites that constantly appears in the New Testament, especially that of light versus darkness, truth versus perfidy, life springing from death, the Kingdom of God versus this world, and the alienation of the community of believers from other men, seems to be derived in large measure from Essenism.

It would be a gross error to suppose that Christianity was merely a variant of Essenism. In the first place, there were significant differences: the Essenes followed the Mosaic law with especial strictness; they were extremely exclusive, as opposed to the desire of Christianity to convert all nations; and they believed that the Messiah would be a military commander who would lead them, the Sons of Light, in victorious battle against the Sons of Darkness (the rest of the world). Essenism was a narrow sect, but Christianity became a broad, often syncretic, universal religion.

Christianity was not a variety of Essenism, but only influenced by it. However, the nature of this influence is extremely important to the subsequent development of the two spirits of order and prophecy. Essenism was strongly colored by a dualism rooted partly in the ancient Canaanite religion (the Canaanites ruled Palestine before the arrival of the Jews and influenced the subsequent development of Jewish religion) and partly in Persian Zoroastrianism. This was a dualist religion postulating a God of Light (Ahura Mazda) and a God of Darkness (Ahriman). These two spirits were independent and fought a constant cosmic struggle that would continue for ages, though Light would eventually triumph over Darkness. It was man's duty to align himself with the forces of Light. This notion seems to have influenced the teaching of Jesus and Paul about the struggle between God and the "Prince of this World," the ruler of an evil eon that would pass in a cataclysm, after which the world would be replaced by the Kingdom of God.

Jesus was ambivalent in his attitude toward the world, sometimes appearing to accept it with the hope of reforming it, in the tradition of orthodox Judaism, and sometimes appearing to reject it utterly, in the tradition of dualism. From the former attitude derives the spirit of order and the notion that Christ came to found a Church that would bring about Christian order in the world; from the latter comes the spirit of prophecy and the determination to cast down and shatter the illusions of this world in order to penetrate immediately to the Kingdom of God. It is precisely this ambivalence that has been the enduring strength of Christianity: it has wholly capitulated neither to the demands of society nor to the cries of fanatics for the overthrow of society.

To this basic balance of forces in Christianity the Greek, as well as the Jewish, tradition, made its contributions. Judea was at the time of Christ a minor province of the Roman Empire, and it was located in that part of the empire that had been heavily Hellenized for three hundred years. Since the time of Alexander the Great the eastern Mediterranean had been bound by the informal but very real ties of Greek civilization. The *Koine,* or common Greek tongue, was the language of commerce, literature, and philosophy throughout Asia Minor, Syria, Egypt, and Palestine, as well as Greece. Alexandria was the greatest center of Greek learning at that time; there the Old Testament was translated into Greek, and there one of the greatest Jewish philosophers, Philo, wrote in the same language. The Gospels and the Epistles were written not in traditional Hebrew or in the Aramaic commonly spoken in the Palestine of apostolic times, but in Greek.

Jesus himself does not seem to have been much influenced by Greek thought, but it is clear that his followers were. They imbibed both the content and the method of Greek philosophy. When St. John wrote, "In the beginning was the Word," he was thinking not only of the Essenic tradition of Wisdom, but of the Platonic and Neoplatonic traditions in which the world is created by a Demiurge or an emanation from the primal God. The *Word* (*Logos* in Greek) is the *Thought* of God by which he creates the universe. This explanation of the nature of the Trinity was spread by later Christian theologians: the Son is the Father's Thought of himself; and the Holy Spirit is the Love which the Father and the Word have for each other.

Ethically, the humane but strict rabbinic morality of Jesus proved very congenial to Stoicism, the most rigorous ethical philosophy current in the Roman Empire. Christian thinkers readily assimilated the rational Stoic principles of moderation and right reason to the revealed principles of the Mosaic and rabbinic laws. Sometimes it became difficult to tell Christian saint from Stoic philosopher, as when St. Clement wrote: "Everything that is contrary to right reason is sin.... Virtue itself is a state of the soul rendered harmonious by reason in respect to the whole life.... And Christian conduct is the operation of the rational soul in accordance with a correct judgment and aspiration after the truth."[1]

Christianity assimilated the method of Greek philosophy even more readily than its content. Christ had left his followers with the impact of his ministry, his death, and his resurrection, but he had not bequeathed any carefully-worked-out system of doctrine. In another cultural context this would not have mattered. Other religions in other places have prospered without a theology: with a fundamentally ethical emphasis, for example, like Con-

[1] St. Clement, "Paedagogus," I, xiii, in Alexander Roberts and James Donaldson, eds., *Ante-Nicene Fathers* (New York, 1890; reprint of Edinburgh edition), Vol. II.

fucianism, Buddhism, and early Judaism; or with a wholly mythological system, like the religions of Babylonia, of Zoroastrian
Persia, or of early Greece and Rome. But Christianity, though it
had mythological underpinnings and was the inheritor of the
strong ethical tradition of Judaism, was not content with these. It
was not content with them because the Hellenistic cultural context
demanded that the questions *why* and *how* be asked, and that an
intellectual system of religion be created by means of rational
reflection upon revelation. This rational reflection, this philosophical investigation of the nature of God and of God's relationship to man, is called theology. St. Paul became the first Christian
theologian when he began constructing a doctrine *about* Christ in
addition to spreading the teachings *of* Christ, and this tradition
was carried on and greatly reinforced by the fathers of the Church,
many of whom were far more intellectual and more Greek in their
way of thought than Paul. This intellectualizing process has
sometimes been called "the Hellenization of Christianity." It has
produced one of Christianity's most distinguishing characteristics:
insistence upon intellectual truth as well as upon right action. One
result was extended investigation of, and often exaggerated debate
on, points of doctrine. But another result was the preservation and
elaboration of the intellectual heritage of Greece that has given
Western civilization a predominant place in the world.

Another kind of Hellenistic influence upon Christianity was
that of the mystery cults, which derived from ancient religions
and were elaborated and syncretized in the Hellenistic civilization
of the eastern Mediterranean. These were fertility cults, uniting
the believer with the deity through certain ceremonial rites and
emphasizing the personal salvation of the individual. At a time
when the old public religion of Rome had ceased to command
widespread belief or support, these religions were making great
headway not only in the East but in Italy and Rome itself. Certain
similarities between them and Christianity have long been
observed. Most of the cults centered upon the ancient myth of the
fertility god or goddess who died and rose again from the dead;
most had a rite of sacrifice and of communion by eating the god's

flesh in a symbolic manner; most taught personal salvation. Mithraism, a religion derived from Zoroastrianism, declared that Mithra, the Son of the Sun, was born of a virgin at the winter solstice (December 25), and the Mithraists had a midnight service to commemorate this nativity—although this particular coincidence is easily explained by the fact that the Church fathers deliberately chose the date of Christmas (no one knew at what time of year Christ was actually born) to discourage Christians from participating in Mithraic rites as well as their own.

Christian writers sometimes borrowed the language and expression of the mystery cults, but Christianity was not merely another of the mystery religions. Their nature was purely mythological and ceremonial; but Christianity had in addition a very advanced ethical and intellectual system. Further, the gods of the mystery religions were generated in some undefined mythical time, while the Christians always took care to press the historical existence of their own founder, who was born in the time of Augustus and who "suffered under Pontius Pilate" in the reign of Tiberius.

But there was one ancient cult which, though indirectly, had enormous influence upon Christianity, and that was Orphism. Orphism was a set of Greek religious ideas existing without formal organization from as early as the eighth century B.C. and named after its legendary founder, Orpheus. Its central myth was that of the god Dionysus. Born as Zagreus, the child of Zeus, the boy was seized by evil Titans and devoured; his father, however, was able to procure his heart and to consume this himself; thereafter Zagreus was reborn again from Zeus as the god Dionysus. Zeus killed the Titans with thunderbolts, and men arose from their ashes—hence men share in both the evil nature of the Titans and in the divine nature of the god whom they had devoured. This myth sets forth the central teaching of Orphism, that *the body is the prison of the soul*: Zagreus-Dionysus is life and spirit; the Titans are the forces of matter, which devour and entrap the spirit; and the resurrection of Dionysus is the salvation of the spirit. The point is that Orphism was a dualistic religion, postulating a conflict between spirit (Good) and matter (Evil).

16

Orphic ideas colored much Greek thought, particularly that of Plato, whose philosophy postulates a dichotomy between a real world of ideas and a less real, illusory, world of matter.

In Christian thought as early as the first century, this Greek dualism was wedded to the Persian dualism derived through the Essenes. The equations were early made in Christian thought that Good is light is spirit and that Evil is darkness is matter or flesh. The world-rejecting aspects of Christianity were thus underscored at the expense of the moderate, world-accepting aspects, and the formation of a strong, sometimes fanatical, distrust of matter and of the body was encouraged. This tradition often burst the bounds of orthodoxy and was condemned as heretical; more often it stayed within the Church, urging it to extremes. It appeared in ancient Gnosticism, Manichaeism, and Montanism, in medieval Reformism and Catharism, in the more extreme practices of monastic asceticism, and in seventeenth-century Jansenism; and it is still manifest in many segments of both Catholic and Protestant Christianity. It attached itself to, and has often discredited, the prophetic spirit. In particular, in its fearful attitude toward sex it cannot be said to have been an altogether healthy or happy aspect of the Christian tradition.

The ideals of Hellenistic kingship came to play a large part in Christian political thought. When Alexander the Great conquered the East and his successors divided it, they adopted the style and manner of the ancient rulers of the East. The Hellenistic ruler was not only an autocrat, as the Great King of Persia had been, but also divine, as Pharaoh had been supposed to be. The awesome qualities of the Hellenistic king were later ascribed, in a modified form, to the Roman emperor. This had two consequences. In the first place, the Christians respected the authority of the emperor, even when he was unjust or unfavorable to Christianity, some of the Church fathers arguing that unjust authority had to be accepted as a punishment visited upon us by God for our sins. In the second place, the majesty of the imperial office persisted, even when the emperors became Christian; and the strong position occupied by the later Byzantine, and to some extent the Holy

17

Roman, emperors in relation to the Church was in this tradition. The idea that in some fashion the emperor had divine authority was a strong element in the medieval conception of order and of the organization of Christian society.

The most important problem of the Church of the first three centuries, apart from its survival in a hostile pagan world, was the development of its doctrine in a way that encouraged discussion and resolution of important points and at the same time discouraged undisciplined speculation that led to heresies and schisms. Even during the lifetime of the apostles, the Christian community was divided between those who wished to hold to the strict dictates of the Mosaic law and those who wished to modify that law to make it easier for the Gentiles to embrace Christianity. By the time the apostles had died, the number of compelling questions and the variety of traditions in the eastern Mediterranean milieu were such that it was impossible to secure a universal consensus.

The greatest difficulty the Christians faced was with the Gnostics. Gnosticism is difficult to define, since it took a great variety of forms. It sprang out of late Judaism at about the same time as Christianity; and like Christianity, it was strongly influenced by Canaanite, Persian, and Greek dualism and by Neoplatonism. Some of the Gnostic sects were purely dualistic; others were closer to Christianity. The Gnostic approach to religion was mythopoeic: the warfare between Good and Evil was clothed in terms of an elaborate cosmogony and cosmology involving intricate generations of gods and demigods. It was difficult for Christianity both to overcome the competition of Gnosticism and to prevent Gnostic doctrines from exercising too great an influence upon Christian believers. In spite of all efforts of the Church fathers to the contrary, some of the Gnostic spirit rubbed off on Christianity,

18

strengthening the otherwordly aspects of the religion. Gnosticism itself remained an independent force in the Middle East, spreading to the Balkans and eventually to western Europe by the twelfth century in the form of Catharism.

Other heresies were provoked by raising the basic issues inherent in the construction of a Christian theology: What is Christian morality and on what basis does it repose? What is the nature of the Trinity? What is the nature of Christ? How is Christian worship to be conducted? What are the sacraments? Is man saved by his own efforts or solely by the will of God?

With this kind of question multiplying, and with the growth of the Christian community in size and importance, it became clear that some kind of system of authority was needed in the Church. The prophetic spirit had created Christianity, but the spirit of order was needed to preserve it. By the end of the third century, in spite of sporadic persecutions, Christianity had spread throughout the Roman Empire and into Persia and India. By 300, a quarter of the population of the eastern half of the empire was Christian, and a tenth of that of the western half. Not only the poor and dispossessed but now some of the nobility and many intellectuals were adhering to the new religion. A pattern of organization had become necessary.

The transformation of the Christian community into an organized Church was the result both of metaphysical and of pragmatic considerations, and it happened very early. Historically, Christianity never really existed as anything other than an "organized religion." At the Last Supper, Christ had already brought the apostles into personal union with him by giving them his body and blood; and St. Paul elaborated the idea that all Christians were one with Christ in a "Mystical Body." Hence the transformation of the community into a corporation (Latin *corpus,* "body") was not wholly an invention of the Middle Ages or even of Roman law. In the earliest years following the Passion of Christ, Christians assumed that the apostles were heirs to his authority, and as the apostles died one by one, their survivors elected new men to fill the empty places. Already in the Book of Acts, Matthias was chosen by the apostles to be of their number. Whoever the apostles consecrated as a successor by the laying on of hands, was deemed to share equally in the responsibility and authority conferred upon the apostles by Christ. This transmission of authority is called apostolic succession, and Orthodox, Catholic, and Anglican bishops today claim that their authority stretches back unbrokenly through the laying on of hands to the time of Christ. Ignatius of Antioch (c. 30–107), one of the greatest Church fathers, had already argued that "we should look upon the bishop even as we would look upon the Lord himself."

The practical need for organization continually increased, and it became necessary to establish rules for the election of the successors of the apostles and to create definitions of the scope and nature of the Church. In the pristine Christian community, there was no distinction between clergy and laity: all were simple followers of the Lord. But almost immediately the Mass, or Lord's Supper, became the center of Christian worship, and some of the community were given the authority to break the bread and offer the cup as Christ had done at the Last Supper. Those who had the power of distributing the sacrament were called indifferently priests (Greek *presbyteroi,* "elders") or bishops (Greek *episkopoi,* "overseers"). Soon it was found useful to have one man in each community with authority to resolve disputes on matters of practice or doctrine, and a distinction was then made between the priests and the bishop. Every important town or city with a Christian community came to have its bishop. Since the largest Christian communities naturally existed in the largest and most important towns of the Roman Empire, it was natural that ecclesiastical organization came to parallel Roman civil administration: the civil administrators and the bishops dwelt in the same towns; and the most important bishops, like the most important administrators, were those who occupied the major cities like Alexandria, Rome, Antioch, or Milan. It was the bishops who generally received consecration from the apostles, and so it was upon the bishops that the powers of the apostolic succession devolved.

At the same time, a definition of the Christian community was necessary. The community was defined as the Church (Greek *ekklesia,* "community," was translated as *ecclesia* in Latin and *church* in English), and the Church was identified with St. Paul's Mystical Body of Christ. All who were joined to Christ in the Mystical Body were saved. But how was membership in the Mystical Body, or indeed in the Church, to be defined? Were all good people members of the Church? But then professed pagans would have to be considered Christians. Were all those who professed belief in Christ members? But there were many, among the Gnostics for example, who claimed to be Christians while teaching eccentric doctrines and even, like Simon Magus, practicing magic. Were only those professed Christians who were pure of heart really members of the Church? This is the idea of the "invisible Church" professed much later by some Protestants, but the difficulty was precisely in building an effective organization out of something invisible.

It therefore became common, though by no means universal, to assume that membership in the Church was limited to those who were in communion with the bishops, the successors of the apostles. St. Ignatius wrote to the Trallians, "Apart from [bishops, priests, and deacons] there is no elect Church, no congregation of holy ones." Through apostolic succession, the bishops had the right to grant Holy Communion to those whom they deemed pure in conduct and correct in doctrine, and otherwise to refuse it. "Let that be deemed a proper Eucharist which is administered by the bishop or by a person whom he has delegated," said Ignatius to the Smyrnans. This was an enormous step toward a principle of order in the Church, and it had an immediate effect upon prophecy. In the earliest years of the Church there were men who imitated Paul and Barnabas by wandering around preaching

Christ to all people. But they were under the authority of no bishop, and some naturally came to teach in an eccentric manner uncongenial to the nascent ecclesiastical authority. Such prophecy was therefore discouraged, and it ceased to exist much beyond the end of the first century.

Indeed, all the organizational developments of which we have been speaking had been effected by the early years of the second century. But several enormous questions remained to be resolved. As the priests and laity in each community had disputed among themselves, so the bishops of the whole Church began to disagree on matters of jurisdiction, of discipline, and of doctrine. Who would be the shepherd of the shepherds and resolve these disputes? Who, in short, constituted the ultimate authority in the Church? The Bible could be no such authority, for it was centuries before a general agreement was reached as to which books it should include, the official canon being set only in 369 by St. Athanasius. There were several possible answers. In the first few centuries, the teachings of the fathers of the Church were given great weight, though of course they frequently disagreed with one another. Public meetings of bishops called synods or councils also had enormous prestige, but there could still be disagreement within the councils; moreover there was the question of who had the authority to call the councils and to select their membership. Then, particular authority came to devolve upon the bishops of those cities most important for their size or for their place in Christian tradition: Jerusalem, Antioch, Alexandria, Rome, and, later, Constantinople. Of these, the bishop of Rome gradually came to be the most important; and much later in the Middle Ages, the bishops of Rome would extend the identification of the Mystical Body with the Church to the Church of Rome, and indeed to the Church of Rome with its governing body, the pope and his cardinals. This was to be the ultimate statement of the principle of order within the Church.

Against growing order, the spirit of prophecy protested. In the first three centuries, when the Christians were often persecuted, the witness of the martyrs was itself an expression of the individual, prophetic spirit. Moreover, there were many who refused to bow to the authority of the bishops in matters of discipline or doctrine and who were therefore expelled from the Church as heretics. Of these, a number were unworthy by virtue of their cowardice in the face of persecution, laxity in morals, or absurdity in doctrine; but there were also many in whom dwelt a righteous prophetic spirit, repulsed by an often narrow and unsympathetic ecclesiastical authority.

Monasticism was the most important of the prophetic movements in the early Church. From the second century it was not uncommon for men, often of wealth and prestige, to withdraw into a desert place to live a life of utter poverty and renunciation. Dressed in rough skins, eating only what they could glean from the often barren land, shunning human comfort and company, they followed the ascetic spirit of John the Baptist or imitated Christ in his own withdrawal for forty days into the desert. Only by renouncing this world completely, these hermits argued, could they wholly fulfill St. Paul's injunction to empty out the self and to install Christ in its place. At first the monks (Greek *monachos,* "one who dwells alone") dwelt each in his complete solitude; but soon the numbers seeking retreat were so many that communities sprang up in the desert; and in order to avoid confusion and anarchy, some sort of rule or order had to be placed even upon the prophets. St. Anthony (d. 356) was the prototype of the hermit; St. Pachomius instituted the first monastic community in 323.

Monasticism has its roots deep in the tradition of Christ. But it is necessary to explain the enormous numbers of men, young and old, who poured into the desert during the third and fourth centuries. It used to be argued that they were fleeing hard times: persecution, economic depression, the general malaise of the later Roman Empire. But this does not suffice. There is no other indication that the depression or malaise was that keenly felt in the population as a whole. An extraordinary proportion of the monks

23

were precisely those men who had wealth and influence in their communities and were the least prone to the effects of moral or economic depression. Finally, the only other period of enormous monastic expansion, in the eleventh and twelfth centuries, is one of great moral and economic advance and optimism. What the two periods, the second and third and the eleventh and twelfth centuries, have in common is that each was a period of rapid growth of organization within the Church. In each era, the advance of the spirit of order called forth a corresponding thrust from the spirit of prophecy. The call of Christ seemed to the monks to demand sacrifice and wholehearted devotion greater even than that preached by the organized Church.

The most spectacular advance of the spirit of order was soon to come. Soon the Roman state, which since the Crucifixion had sporadically prosecuted and persecuted Christianity, would adopt a new policy of tolerance. Soon the divine emperor himself would lay claim to being the supreme authority over the Christian Church. Soon, through the Christianization of the empire, the spirit of order would be able to equate the Church with society as a whole and to strive to build on earth a *societas christiana*, a Christian society.

The Peace
of
the Church

The "Peace of the Church"—the end of persecution by the Roman state and people—transformed the problems and even the nature of Christianity. Though the persecutions had been sporadic, and though their ferocity has sometimes been exaggerated (Nero probably did not, for example, use Christians as human torches to illuminate his nocturnal revels), they were harsh enough and deeply rooted in popular support. They were mostly launched, not by official decree, but by the fanaticism of the people. Christianity was at once despised by the intellectual and cultured as an absurd doctrine suitable only to the vulgar, and loathed by the vulgar as something strange and, therefore, obscene. In some sort of dark psychological process, people have always accused little-known religions of heinous crimes, particularly sexual orgies and child-murder or cannibalism. Some southern Protestants still charge Catholics with such crimes; Christians have so accused Jews; medieval Catholics the heretics; and the Roman people the Christians. Christianity seemed wicked or detestable, and the earliest depiction of the Crucifixion we possess is a graffito of a crucified donkey with the mocking inscription "Alexamenos [evidently a local Christian] adores his god." But the most serious charge leveled against the Christians, one which enlisted State support for the persecutions, was that of atheism.

The charge of atheism was made in deadly earnest. The religion of ancient Rome, as indeed the religion of most societies, was public and official in nature. The Romans and the Greeks knew no distinction between religion and the State, between devotion to the public cult and patriotism. Every Roman was required to perform certain public acts of devotion to the gods; what he believed in his own home was up to him. It was a state very tolerant of a variety of private religious practices as long as the public manifestations of patriotism were retained. Most religions found no objections to this point of view, which had been normal for millennia. Only a few refused to offer public sacrifice; of these the Christians were the most numerous. Their reasoning was simple: there was but one God, and he had commanded them to have no other gods but him. But to the Roman state and people, disloyalty to the gods of Rome bespoke disloyalty to the Roman state. In vain did the Christians fulfill all the other duties of citizenship, including military service; in vain did they plead that their high morality made them even better citizens than the ordinary. They would not sacrifice to the gods, and so they were traitors.

Persecutions flared up here and there throughout the empire, but in the third century they expanded in scope and thoroughness. After the Christians spurned the generous offer of the Emperor Aurelian (270–275) to include Christ in the pantheon along with Mithra as a manifestation of the Unconquered Sun, the State determined to root out these subversives. It was the best emperors, those who were most energetic in trying to pull together the weakening bonds of Roman society, who could least tolerate the Christians' refusal to submit totally to the imperial will. So the great Diocletian, whose persecution began in 303, and his successors Maxentius (d. 312) and Galerius (d. 311) launched the most merciless pogroms of all.

Though many Christians lapsed, many suffered bravely under persecution and by their example converted many more. As the moralist Tertullian (fl. 190–210) remarked, "the blood of the martyrs was the seed of the Church." Most of the Church fathers taught that the proper attitude toward persecution was passive obedience, in recognition that it came from God as the just punishment of sin.

This passive acceptance of what Christians considered a bad order of society became an active acceptance of a good order of society when the persecutions stopped and a new era of tolerance was ushered in by Constantine the Great.

Constantine was born in Britain of a soldier father, Constantius Chlorus, and a Christian mother, St. Helena. Helena later claimed to have been successful in discovering in Palestine the remnants of the True Cross upon which Jesus had died, but her success in making her son a Christian was less marked. During the political and military upheavals following the retirement of Diocletian as emperor in 305, the empire was divided, and Constantine's father laid claim to the imperial title in the West. He died before he could recognize his ambitions, but he bequeathed them to his son. The legions stationed in Britain proclaimed Constantine emperor, and he proceeded to engage his rivals in a series of battles from which, with the help of his ally Licinius, he emerged victorious. Eventually he also deposed Licinius and assumed the rule of the entire empire in 324.

It has long been debated whether Constantine was a Christian. The Church father Lactantius tells a story that was adapted by Constantine's biographer, Eusebius, and entered into popular belief: Before the battle of the Milvian Bridge, in which Constantine defeated one of his rivals and thus was able to occupy the city of Rome, he is supposed to have seen the symbol ⳇ in the sky (XP, the first letters of the name Christ in Greek) with a legend in Greek which translated into Latin is, *in hoc signo vinces*, "by this sign shalt thou conquer." In fact it is not only doubtful whether Constantine saw the vision, but whether he was ever really a Christian at all. As emperor he continued the public religion of Rome, with special attention to the Unconquered Sun; he struck coins and medals in honor of the Sun and other deities, including himself as divine emperor. If he ever formally professed Christianity, it was probably not until he was on his deathbed.

Nonetheless the reign of Constantine marked a great advance in Christian fortunes. In the decade 310–320, Constantine, Licinius, and even the dying and repentant Galerius issued a number of edicts in which persecutions of the Christians were halted, tolerance of all religious beliefs and practices was proclaimed, the obligation of public sacrifice was lifted, and the authority of Christian bishops was recognized. Constantine did not establish Christianity as a state religion, but whether from religious motives or for reasons of state, he favored it above the others as he grew older. He seems to have recognized that it was becoming the most numerous and influential cult in the empire. In any event, the age of persecution was over, and the age of Constantine began: the age of alliance of Church with State that has endured in at least some countries into the twentieth century.

To some Christians, notably Eusebius of Caesarea, the admiring chronicler of the deeds of Constantine, the alliance of Christianity with the empire was natural. There was a theory of history derived from the Hellenistic period in which four or five universal monarchies succeeded one another in progression. Some of the Christian fathers like Irenaeus and Tertullian affirmed that the Roman Empire was the last and greatest of the universal monarchies and that its fall would bring about the appearance of the Antichrist, dreadful war and ruin, and the end of the world. Because of this theory, as well as because many Christians assumed implicitly, like their pagan fellow-Romans, that Rome was eternal, there was universal consternation and horror when Rome actually did fall to the barbarians in 410. A hundred years earlier, at the time of Constantine, Eusebius and other Christians believed that the preservation of the Roman state was necessary for the preservation of the world and that the union of Christianity and the empire under Constantine and his successors was wholly desirable.

The effects of this union—the Peace of the Church—were several. In the first place the Christian community was relieved of a great dread and fear. It was now possible to practice Christianity without danger to life or limb. Yet even this was a mixed blessing. Heretofore only those with strong convictions had entered the Church, which had been a community of martyrs and heroes of whom even some pagan writers observed that they stood out from the population by virtue of their morality and their acts of love and mercy. Now the lukewarm diluted the fervor of the Christian community even while swelling its numbers.

Further, after Constantine made it legal to bequeath property to the Church, and as the emperor gradually came to prefer Christians over pagans for promotions in the army and the civil service, the Church grew rich and powerful. As one modern theologian, Hans Küng, has put it, "this was worse than a persecution." Not only the lukewarm but also the timeservers now entered the Church, which became a road to advancement within society more than a tribunal of judgment upon society. As the Church grew wealthier, corrupt practices like simony (the sale or purchase of the sacraments or of ecclesiastical offices) became more common. The history of medieval Christianity really begins with the Age of Constantine, for it was then that the intricate involvement of the Church with the State began, with all of its dilemmas. Few people in the Church resisted this new dispensation, in which the order of society was identified with the order of the Church. They were too relieved to escape persecution; they were too eager to Christianize society by the use of political influence; and they were too accustomed to the formal attachment of religion to the State. The idea of real religious pluralism was almost inconceivable to a religion that was convinced that it possessed the only ethical and metaphysical truth.

The effects, both good and dubious, of the alliance of Christianity with the State appeared immediately. On the one hand, the involvement of the Church in politics significantly modified the laws and customs of society. Through their influence, Christians checked the degeneration of sexual mores that was threatening the family, one of the basic institutions of classical Rome. They put an end to the hideous spectacles in which men and animals tortured one another to death in the colosseums to the screaming delight of a brutal mob. They were able to modify the totalitarian notion of the State so common in both ancient and very modern times and, at least to some degree, to introduce morality into the practice of politics. These are no mean achievements, witness the greater inhumanity of politics in societies in which religion has not taken part in politics or where, as in Nazi Germany or some of the Communist countries, its influence has been distorted or removed.

Yet, on a deeper level, some accommodation of the Church to society was necessary. A religion that through exaggerated conservatism ceases to express the true life of the community or ceases to speak in a language which the community can understand condemns itself to isolation and eventual impotence or even extinction. The ability of Christianity to adapt to society at the same time as it adapted society to itself is one of the secrets of its long endurance.

But for these advantages medieval Christianity paid a price. The acquisition of political power and influence invited, indeed almost demanded, interference on the part of any energetic ruler determined to secure order by the use of every tool at his disposal. For Constantine and his successors, the Church became such a tool.

Perceiving that the balance of wealth, population, and power had shifted to the East, Constantine determined to build a new capital at Byzantium, a second Rome which he adorned with all the splendors of the first. He renamed the city Constantinople, took up his residence there, and caused its episcopate to be elevated to the level of the four other patriarchates, Rome, Alexandria, Jerusalem, and Antioch. He prepared a shrine for the twelve apostles in which he caused to be erected a thirteenth tomb reserved for himself; and his biographer Eusebius bestowed upon him the title of "Equal of the Apostles." Apparently convinced that the Church was the chief unifying force in the empire, Constantine not only patronized it but undertook to direct it. The first great ecumenical council, that of Nicaea in 325, was summoned and presided over not by a patriarch, but by the emperor, who even intervened in the theological discussions and used the authority of the State to compel assent to doctrinal decisions. It was at this council that the Arians, followers of the Alexandrian priest Arius who argued that the Father was superior to the Son and Holy Ghost, were condemned. When Constantine died in 337, he had already established the tradition of "caesaropapism," in which the chief authority over the Church is supposed to be delegated by God directly to the emperor.

Constantine's successors were even less reticent. Now openly Christians, they argued imperial authority in the Church with all the conviction that material force and influence could lend. Though some supported one side of the great doctrinal controversies of the time and some the other, they all argued that it was the emperor who was entitled to determine what was orthodox; and the Emperor Constantius went so far as to declare that "whatever I will must have the force of ecclesiastical law." The alliance between Church and State was finally sealed in 391 under the Emperor Theodosius the Great, who formally established Christianity as the official religion of the empire and outlawed paganism. The tables were turned, and the religion that had suffered persecution with patient dignity now eagerly encouraged stiff civil penalties for paganism and for heresy. In such a Church the prophetic spirit found expression increasingly difficult.

Prophetic resistance to these trends sometimes took extreme

31

forms. The first conflict between extreme purists and moderates took place even before the reign of Constantine. During the great persecutions at the end of the third century and the beginning of the fourth, many Christians had nominally abjured Christianity in order to save their lives. When the persecutions were over, they sought to return to the Church. The majority of the faithful were willing to accept them, but a minority refused, condemning the cowards as apostates. The extremists' greatest strength was in the province of Africa and in neighboring Numidia, where they were called Donatists after their bishop, Donatus. The Donatists refused to recognize any bishop or priest who had apostasized, however temporarily, and they even condemned anyone who was willing to be in communion with such alleged cowards. Donatism spread widely and persisted until the Vandal conquest of Roman Africa in 429, a conquest hastened by the bitter feuds between Catholics and Donatists. Perhaps the most important significance of Donatism is that it represented a reaction of purists against worldly compromise that became typical of many protest movements within the Church down to the present. Many medieval heretics, though unconnected with historical Donatism, held identical beliefs, refusing to accept the validity of sacraments administered by an immoral priest, as against the teaching of the Church that sacerdotal powers were independent of the worthiness of the priest.

In the meantime, the establishment of order within the Church was growing. By the end of the fourth century, when Christianity was established as the official religion of the empire, the majority of the Roman population were nominally Christian. The new religion had first spread to the Jewish communities of the commercial cities of the Mediterranean, and then to all the people of those cities. The peasants in the hinterland, always conservative, clung longer to the old ways: the word "pagan" originally meant "country-dweller." By 400, when even the country people had been converted, there was need to expand and modify the pristine organization of the Church. In the beginning, there had been no organization of the dioceses into parishes, the priests living instead at large in the city or with the bishop. By the fourth century, the growing numbers of Christian people and the growing stability and wealth of the Church made it possible to build several churches in every major town. The chief of these churches was called the cathedral (Latin *cathedra,* "chair," i.e., the chair where the bishop sat) and was designated the bishop's residence. The other churches were usually designated parish churches, and each was in the charge of a priest. Large and important churches would be staffed by several priests, the leader of whom was called the rector or pastor. The older system, in which the priests of the diocese all lived together with their bishop, continued to be used in wild and newly converted areas. During the conversion of the English, for example, the priests of a diocese lived with the bishop in his "minster." The English countryside, as yet devoid of parish churches, was studded with rude stone crosses, to which the priests of the minster would journey as often as circumstances permitted in order to say Mass for the faithful. In the East, and sometimes in the West, bishops chose *chorepiscopi,* "country-bishops," as auxiliaries in rural areas, but this custom slowly disappeared.

As more territory was Christianized, the number of dioceses grew. In the East, it was common for even smaller towns to have their bishops; in the West, only major cities were generally made into episcopal sees. The official recognition of Christianity made it natural to draw the boundary lines of the dioceses to correspond roughly with Roman administrative boundaries. As smaller Roman administrative units were grouped into larger, so it also became the custom in the Church to group dioceses into larger units called provinces. The Council of Nicaea of 325 urged bishops to gather periodically in provincial councils in order to discuss common problems and to coordinate policies. The bishop of the most important metropolis in the province (like Rome, Milan, Alexandria, or Lyon) was called the metropolitan bishop, and it was his authority to call the provincial synods and to preside over them. Thus the beginnings of a hierarchy were established: the priest of the parish was responsible to the bishop of the diocese, and the bishop of the diocese to the metropolitan of the province.

There were in the fourth and fifth centuries two obstacles to further elaboration of the hierarchy. First, the bishops were the successors of the apostles. As no authority higher than apostolic authority was conceivable, there was consecration to no higher office than that of bishop. The metropolitans remained bishops, and as a result their authority over other bishops was always tenuous and disputed. By the seventh century the institution of metropolitans gradually faded away. Second, the authority of the civil power, particularly that of the emperor, made itself so strongly felt as to inhibit the growth of any other authority over the entire Church. In the fourth and fifth centuries there were two major possibilities for such authority: the bishops of the great patriarchal sees and the ecumenical councils.

After the establishment of Constantinople, there were five patriarchal sees. From the end of the first century at least, these sees were accustomed to receive requests from lesser communities for advice and arbitration. In about 95, for example, the Church of Corinth asked the Church of Rome to help resolve a local dispute. Of the five patriarchs, those of Rome and Constantinople emerged preeminent by the fourth century because of their location in the seats of empire. Even their power was inhibited both by the influence of the emperors and also by an ancient rule against the transfer of bishops from one diocese to another. This meant that the ablest bishops of minor sees had no chance of being elevated to the patriarchate and that upon entering into their office the patriarchs had no episcopal experience. Nevertheless the growth of the power of the patriarchs of Rome and Constantinople was impressive.

That of Constantinople was the more striking in that the city was of little importance until Constantine made it his capital, yet in 381 the Council of I Constantinople conferred upon the patriarch a primacy in honor second only to that of Rome. Though

Alexandria was the most venerable see of the East, it found its power gradually slipping to that of Constantinople, which enjoyed special imperial patronage, the prestige of the capital, and the advantage of being near when dignitaries and bishops from all over the empire came to call upon their ruler. Yet the very presence of the emperor proved in the long run disadvantageous. Constantinople enjoyed immense ecclesiastical power; but that power was more often imperial than patriarchal, and the bishop of the Second Rome, patronized and often appointed by the emperor, was obliged to be obedient to his master. It was not the patriarch but the Emperor Constantine who called the First Nicene Council, the Emperor Theodosius who issued edicts against pagans and heretics, and the Emperor Justinian who erected the great cathedral of Hagia Sophia.

The rise of the bishops of Rome was less spectacular but more enduring. In the first place, they had the advantage of certain theoretical claims to primacy. When Christ bestowed authority upon the apostles, he appears to have given Peter preeminence (see, for example, Matthew 16:17–19). Since Peter journeyed to Rome, probably led the Christian community there, and was finally crucified there, the bishops of Rome could claim that they were his successors. They argued that they had inherited not only the general authority of the apostles but the special authority of Peter.

It is now no longer necessary to dispute at length over the pristine powers of the bishop of Rome. Old-fashioned Catholics used to imagine that they were obliged to argue that the popes of the second century exercised, at least implicitly, the same plenitude of power accorded Pius IX in 1870; old-fashioned Protestants supposed that they had only to disprove this in order to demonstrate that the institution of the papacy was fraudulent. Neither argument is particularly cogent. The early papacy certainly did not possess anything remotely resembling its later powers; but these powers were gradually acquired through a process of development typical of many historical institutions. Whether or not this development was metaphysically legitimate is a question for the theologian, not the historian.

In the development of papal powers there were several conceptual as well as chronological stages. Conceptually, the papacy first obtained recognition of its primacy in honor throughout the Church. Second, it obtained the right to judge disputes submitted to it by other dioceses. Third, it gradually obtained the right to administer the Church as a whole in matters of jurisdiction and discipline. Fourth, it gradually secured the right to define doctrine. Fifth, for a while it even claimed the right to rule all of Christian society not only in spiritual but even in temporal matters.

Chronologically, the acquisition of these powers is difficult to define, for it was full of false starts and retreats as well as gradual progress. To begin with, the bishop of Rome had several advantages in addition to his theoretical primacy. First, he occupied the ancient capital of the empire and so even here had the upper hand over his brother at Constantinople. Second, the imperial power in Rome declined markedly over the centuries. For most of the fourth century there was no emperor in Rome at all, and Constantinople was responsible for the entire empire. In the fifth century there were emperors at Rome until 476, but their powers were greatly reduced by the effects of internal dissensions and the barbarian invasions. After 476, Constantinople resumed the sole rule of the empire, but, except for the time of Justinian (527–565) and his immediate successors, it was unable to exert direct control over much of Italy. There were certain handicaps to being away from the center of civil power, but on the positive side the opportunities for independent action were greater. The imperial presence did not overshadow the bishop of Rome as it did the bishop of Constantinople. The popes pursued a policy independent of, and sometimes antagonistic to, that of the emperor; and if Rome remained the Eternal City, it did so because of the prestige of the papacy, not that of the empire. Finally, while the

East had three patriarchates (including the powerful Alexandria) that rivaled Constantinople, Rome was the only patriarchate in the West. Aside from the bishop of Carthage, who enjoyed great prestige throughout Africa, Rome was without a rival in fully half of the empire, and the fall of Carthage in 439 to the heretical Vandals enhanced the position of Rome even more. In the second century, St. Irenaeus (120–202) is supposed to have said, "It is a matter of necessity that every Church should agree with this Church [of Rome], on account of its preeminent authority."[1] Pope Victor (189–198) intervened in Asia to order the churches there to conform to the Roman date of Easter. Pope Siricius (385–399) established a papal vicariate in Thessalonica.

Yet as late as 400, papal powers were very ill defined. In the first ecumenical council the papacy and the West as a whole were scarcely represented. More common than theories of papal primacy were those of episcopal collegiality: St. Cyprian (200–258) argued that it was upon the episcopate *as a whole* that the Church was founded and that the bishops *as a whole* were the supreme authority in the Church. This argument found many supporters until the triumph of papal monarchy in the eleventh century. It has always been held by the Eastern Orthodox Church, and it has been revived since, by the conciliar movement of the fifteenth century, by Anglican and Lutheran Protestants, and, to a limited extent, even by the Roman Catholic Church at the time of the Second Vatican Council of 1962–1965.

It was really owing to the labors of a few great popes of the fifth and sixth centuries that the power of the papacy in the West was firmly established. The first of these was Pope Leo the Great (440–461), who ruled Rome while the Western empire was coming rapidly to an end. The Visigoths had already taken the Eternal City (410) and passed on to southern Gaul and Spain. The Franks occupied northern Gaul; the Vandals had conquered

---

[1]There is much disagreement as to what Irenaeus meant by the term *principalis,* which is here translated "preeminent." Certainly Irenaeus had nothing in mind as definite or far-reaching as the *principatus* claimed by Gelasius I, Gregory I, and later popes.

Africa and the Anglo-Saxons much of Britain. Only Italy remained to the empire, and there the imperial military forces, from the lowest infantryman to the commander-in-chief, consisted almost entirely of barbarian mercenaries. The moral authority of the emperor was even more tenuous. Into this situation burst the Huns, a pagan, savage group of conquerors from the plains of central Asia, their powers recently united under one ruler, the bloodthirsty Attila. After ravaging the Balkans and central Europe, Attila invaded Gaul, where he was defeated by an alliance of Romans, Burgundians, Franks, and Visigoths at the decisive battle of the Catalaunian Plains (or battle of Châlons) in 451. Repulsed from Gaul, Attila invaded Italy and from Milan announced his intention of conquering Rome itself. Helpless to prevent the conquest by military force, the emperor abdicated his responsibility to the pope.

As the power of the emperor and the Roman civil administration decayed in the West, it had in part passed to the bishops, who were the only other authorities of note in the cities. In many localities the bishop had been entrusted with the civil, financial, and even military administration of the town. In Rome similar powers passed to Leo from the hands of an impotent emperor. It was Leo who led the embassy to meet the tired and aging Attila in Milan and there persuaded him by means of a sizable tribute to refrain from his projected conquest. It was Leo who took charge of the repair of the fortifications of Rome and the repair of the public buildings. In all this, Leo was appropriating to the papacy a certain temporal authority.

Leo's prestige was not limited to administrative affairs or to the West alone. When he intervened in the doctrinal dispute between the Nestorians and the Monophysites and persuaded the Council of Chalcedon (451) to accept as orthodox his definition of the nature of Christ, it was the first time that a pope had exercised such influence at a general council. When his letter was read to the assembled bishops, they agreed that "this is the faith of the Fathers; this is the faith of the Apostles. This is the faith of us all. Peter has spoken through Leo."

It is his insistence upon the pope's role as the successor of Peter that makes Leo one of the earliest proponents of a Christian order dominated by the papacy. Leo was the first pope to argue that the pope was the vicar of Peter: that he had the right to rule the Church as the Fisherman's successor. It was he who for the first time emphasized that Christ had given the keys and the power to bind and loose to Peter alone. Just as Peter in turn had delegated these powers to the other apostles, so the pope delegated power to the other bishops. The next step, which would not be taken until the papacy had reached its zenith, would be to state that Peter and his successors functioned as vicars of Christ. The superiority in honor over other bishops of Peter's successors was accepted by the Council of Chalcedon, but that body also promoted an idea of order somewhat different from Leo's. It declared that the see of Constantinople, though second to Rome in honor, was equal in rank and power, and it affirmed that even as Rome had authority over the West, so Constantinople had authority over Pontus, Thrace, and the province of Asia. This idea would have great consequence, eventually dividing Christendom into two orders and two societies: Roman Catholicism and Eastern Orthodoxy.

Gelasius I (492–496) pressed the claims of the papacy further. The Emperor Zeno attempted to impose upon the Church his own doctrine of Christ's nature, but Gelasius responded to this effort and to that of Zeno's successor, the Emperor Anastasius I, by asserting the independence and indeed the supremacy of the priestly authority. It was the pope's function to teach, and the emperor's to learn, what was the good in society. As successor of Peter, the pope had authority over all of Christian society, and the emperor was only his helper, if a most important one. This Gelasian doctrine was often cited and much developed by the papalists in the long struggle between papacy and empire in the later Middle Ages.

The most important pope of the early Middle Ages was Gregory I the Great (590–604). Born into a noble Roman family, Gregory first pursued a career in civil administration, but as a young man he perceived the contradiction between the teachings of Christ and the pursuit of wealth and prestige. He withdrew from the world and established a monastic community on his family property. But he could not remain long in isolation. His reputation as an administrator of rectitude and skill was too great, and he was persuaded to return to public life in the ecclesiastical administration of the city. Elected pope in 590, he continued the policies of Leo the Great, acting as the emperor's representative in the city of Rome, collecting taxes, providing for welfare, arming and training soldiers, repairing public buildings and fortifications, and taking chief responsibility for the defense of Roman interests against the invading Lombards, who were both barbarians and Arian heretics. By exercising these powers and by adding to the papal patrimony (land owned directly by "St. Peter" —i.e., the papacy), he increased the temporal power of the papacy.

A clear and cogent theologian and political theorist, Gregory did not confine his talents merely to administration and to Italy. He was one of the greatest architects of medieval order. The foundation of his theory of Christian society was that it must imitate or reflect heavenly society. As heaven was organized hierarchically, each spirit in his proper place and rank, so Christendom must be. St. Augustine had already written, "Order is an arrangement assigning their proper places to equal and unequal things"; and Gregory added, "Universal society could subsist by no other principle than that of a great system of order preserving its diversity of operations." Order not only establishes tranquillity and unity, but it preserves and protects the right of each person and each creature to occupy his proper place and to fulfill the functions assigned him by God. Gregory argued that in practice, order was to be achieved by the construction of a chain of command linking priest to bishop to pope. Such notions of hierarchical order became the basis of the unified and structured organization of the Church that progressed from the eighth century and culminated in the political theories of Gregory VII in the eleventh.

With such a view, Gregory I could not but contest the dispensation of Chalcedon, which divided Rome's authority with Constantinople. The pope made a practice of hearing appeals against the patriarch on the part of Eastern clergy; in theory he objected openly to the patriarch's use of the term "universal bishop." This term implied a universal authority on the part of Constantinople that properly, Gregory argued, pertained only to the Roman see, which has *principatus*—authority—over the whole Church.

It was the desire to establish order, with the *principatus* and the hierarchical organization it entailed, that led Gregory to initiate what was perhaps his most significant policy: the extension of papal influence and prestige north of the Alps. Until that time northern Europe had formally recognized the primacy of Rome while paying little attention to papal decrees. With extraordinary vigor, witnessed by his voluminous correspondence, Gregory now intervened in the affairs of local churches everywhere. In 595–597 he launched the conversion of the English to Roman Catholicism by sending St. Augustine of Canterbury to convert Kent and to establish the see of Canterbury. The English eventually became the strongest supporters of the papacy in the north, and in the eighth century their missionaries to the Continent would do much to establish papal authority in Gaul and Germany.

At Gregory's death in 604, conditions both in the Church and in society as a whole were still unsettled, but the papacy had become a leading force for order. It had developed the potential for becoming the center and focus of an orderly *societas christiana*, a potential that would be further actualized by a succession of great popes in the eighth century.

Another great force for order in the Church was the ecumenical council. Yet the ecumenical council has always had the weakness of depending for its direction upon whatever authority summoned it. The early councils were all called by emperors and were closely bound to imperial policy. Constantine and his successors called general councils to remove dissension and to promote unity; this they did for the welfare of the State as well as the Church. Accordingly, the councils addressed themselves primarily to healing doctrinal and jurisdictional disputes.

The first major doctrinal dispute in the Church concerned the nature of the Trinity. Christ had spoken both of his Father and of the Holy Spirit but had not defined their functions. The Christian community from its inception believed in a divine Trinity—Father, Son, and Holy Spirit—but there was no general agreement as to the function of the Three Persons. Most of the early fathers of the Church were subordinationists, believing that the Son and the Holy Spirit were subordinate in time and in power to the Father. The consensus, however, moved in the direction of considering the Three Persons equal in every respect, so that by 300 the subordinationist position had become old-fashioned. When, therefore, a priest and theologian of Alexandria, Arius, openly defended a variety of subordinationism, he was roundly attacked and eventually excommunicated by his bishop. Arius's chief opponent was a deacon of Alexandria named Athanasius, and soon Christians, particularly in the East, were divided into an Arian and an Athanasian party. Constantine summoned the First Council of Nicaea in 325 to deal with the question, and the assembled Church fathers, after lengthy debate, approved the Athanasian position.

Arianism did not perish with the Nicene Council, however. Some of the successors of Constantine were themselves Arian and not only supported Arianism at home but encouraged Arian missionaries. These missionaries were successful in converting many of the barbarian tribes, notably the Ostrogoths, Visigoths, Vandals, Burgundians, and Lombards, so that all of these people were Arians at the time of their irruption into the empire. A second ecumenical council (I Constantinople 381) confirmed the decisions of Nicaea and approved the Nicene Creed in the form still recited in churches. The emperor Theodosius embraced the Catholic (Athanasian) position and proscribed the Arians as heretics. But Arianism remained a potent force in the barbarian kingdoms of the West into the seventh century.

The second great doctrinal dispute concerned the nature of Christ. Everyone agreed that Christ was the Son of God, but what did this mean? The school of Antioch and its followers, notably Nestorius, patriarch of Constantinople from 428, argued that Jesus had both two natures and two separate persons: one person was wholly human and the other person wholly divine. Mary, in consequence, was not the "Mother of God," of the divine Christ, but only the mother of the human Jesus. The Nestorians were condemned at the third ecumenical council (Ephesus, 431); but some of their opponents, particularly the school of Alexandria, went to extremes and argued that Christ had but one person and one nature, the divine. This was known as the *monophysite* ("one nature") position and was condemned at the fourth ecumenical council (Chalcedon, 451) on the grounds that it ignored the humanity of Christ. At Chalcedon the teaching of Pope Leo the Great was accepted as orthodox: Christ is but one person, but that person has two natures, the human and the divine. This doctrine was confirmed at the fifth ecumenical council (II Constantinople, 553), though both the Nestorians and the Monophysites remained strong, particularly in Syria and Egypt. The present Coptic Church of Egypt is Monophysite, and the Nestorians were such effective missionaries in Persia and central Asia during the Middle Ages that they converted many tribes and established churches as far east as Mongolia and China.

The most significant aspect of the conflict between the Nestorians and the Monophysites is the way in which it illustrates the development of doctrine. At first there had been an open question: the exact nature of Christ. On this question there had been for centuries a variety of opinions. After much consideration, by the fifth century two of these opinions emerged as cogent and popular. The question was publicly raised and debated; a council made a decision and defined a doctrine. In the Arian dispute, the Church affirmed one side of the question; in the argument between Nestorians and Monophysites it took a compromise position. In both cases, once the question was resolved and an official doctrine proclaimed publicly, only those who affirmed that doctrine were considered orthodox; others were condemned as heretics. In this way Christian doctrine grew; in this way too the intellectual emphasis of Christianity—the search for metaphyscal truth—was confirmed.

The exercise of imperial power, the growth of the papacy and of diocesan organization, the definition of doctrine, the acquisition by the Church of political influence in society as a whole, all these were signs of a growing Christian order that was soon wholly to supplant the order of classical Rome.

The Mind of the Church, 300–700

Order and prophecy both found a place in the intellectual and cultural expression of the early medieval Church, but it was the spirit of order that generally prevailed in the formation of Christian doctrine, under the influence of Greek philosophy. Doctrine was formed not only by the decisions of bishops and councils but, more basically, through reflection upon the ethical and metaphysical implications of Christianity on the part of theologians.

The first four centuries of the Church constitute, in terms of Christian intellectual formation, the age of the Church fathers, teachers who first systematically elaborated these implications. The higher schools of the Roman Empire, like the Academy in Athens, were long dominated by pagans, and the Christian intellect had to find expression outside the classical system of education. Till the middle of the second century, the so-called "Apostolic Fathers" usually taught in the Jewish manner. Beginning with Justin Martyr, who was converted about 130, the "Apologist Fathers," in defense against the philosophical assaults of their pagan antagonists, adopted both the method and the matter of classical civilization. The adoption of philosophy by the Christians was hastened by the conversion of pagan philosophers like Justin, and by the demand for an antidote against the intellectual heresy of Gnosticism. The resulting wedding of reason and revelation was fruitful for the development of Christianity as a vehicle of thought and culture.

Justin was born to a pagan Greek family in Samaria about 110; he received a classical education and determined, in the classical manner, to seek out truth. He became in turn a Stoic, a Peripatetic, and a Pythagorean, but no system seemed to him adequately sophisticated. He was surprised to find that sophistication in Christianity, which all intellectuals were supposed to disdain. In a great book, *Conversion*,[1] Arthur Darby Nock chose Justin's as the model of one of the three types of conversion, the intellectual quest— the other two being a sense of personal sin and disgust with the state of society. Justin's significance is that, unlike most earlier converts from Greek paganism, he did not feel an obligation to reject his classical background altogether. Rather than sneering at the limitations of the antique philosophers, Justin argued that their teachings were in many ways parallel to those of Jesus and that they therefore, like the writers of the Old Testament, must have received some seminal divine inspiration.

Many Christian writers, like Tertullian (145–220), remained very suspicious of the classics. Even Justin's pupil Tatian (110–172) held that the Greek philosophers were all vain boasters and the Greek gods all demons. But the attitude of Athenagoras (fl. 177–180), who searched not only the philosophers but the poets for presentiments of divine truth, was becoming more common. Christian doctrine was becoming increasingly a synthesis of Greek with Jewish thought. St. Irenaeus (120–202) may have been the first systematic theologian, combining Scripture with careful philosophical reasoning in order to refute the heretics of his day.

Typical of the efforts to reconcile Judeo-Christian revelation with Greek rationalism was the development by the school of Alexandria of the allegorical method of interpretation of the

[1]London, 1933.

Bible, an approach that was to have immeasurable influence on medieval literature as well as theology. It was at Alexandria that the Jewish philosopher Philo had first applied it to the understanding of the Old Testament. For Philo, the problem was this: the Scriptures are the revealed word of God; yet the revered patriarchs and kings of the Old Testament often behaved in a fashion difficult to reconcile with right reason. Jacob defrauded Esau, Lot slept with his daughters, and David seduced Bathsheba and sent her husband off to be killed. Even Yahweh seemed on occasion vengeful, cruel, or even whimsical. In order to preserve intact both revelation and reason, Philo concluded that the Scriptures must have a meaning other than that of the literal. For example, when Isaac was obliged to marry Leah in preparation for taking to wife his beloved Rachel, this is to be interpreted, said Philo, as the necessity for the student to undertake preliminary studies before devoting himself to understanding divine revelation.

Such ideas were embraced by the Christian teachers Clement of Alexandria (153–217) and his pupil Origen (185–254). Similar approaches have always been followed throughout the Church except by fundamentalist Protestants of the last few centuries, who insisted that the Bible was absolutely true in the literal sense.

Origen was born at Alexandria to devout Christian parents. As a young child he showed such interest in theology that his father, Leonides, became convinced that the child was the special dwelling place of the Holy Spirit. When the persecution launched by the Emperor Septimius Severus deprived Leonides of both his property and his life, Origen, the eldest of eleven children, undertook to support them by teaching grammar and literature. His devotion to theology matured with his talents, and he was ordained to the priesthood and appointed head of the cathedral school of Alexandria; but his brilliance was matched by a stubbornness that provoked the ecclesiastical leaders of the city. He was defrocked and spent the remainder of his life in exile in Caesarea. His writings are voluminous and original. His greatest contribution was the further elucidation of the allegorical method of interpreting the Scriptures.

Both Testaments of the Bible are the work of God and the Holy Spirit, Origen argued, but the real meaning of the Old Testament is less in its literal signification than in its hidden meaning, which becomes clear only after being illuminated by the new revelation of Jesus and by the principles of philosophy. The Old Testament is to be understood on several levels, of which Origen originally specified three. St. Augustine used four, which came in the Middle Ages to be accepted as standard: the historical, the etiological (moral), the analogical (the Old Testament seen as prefiguring the New), and the allegorical. For example, the story of Joshua at the battle of Jericho means (1) literally and historically, that Joshua took Jericho; (2) morally, that the walls of sin will crumble before the man of faith; (3) analogically, that Jesus entered Jerusalem in triumph; (4) allegorically, that on the Last Day the world will crumble when the trumpet of judgment sounds. Not only did medieval theologians search the Old Testament for such meanings, but they carefully composed their own works on several planes. The poets and historians took up the method; and in the *Divine Comedy,* Dante, as he explained to his friend Can Grande della Scala, carefully used the four levels of meaning. This complex pattern of thought and expression was woven into the fabric of medieval Christian culture.

After the Peace of the Church, the great schools of the empire were opened to the Christians, but the schools themselves had deteriorated considerably from the days of Plato and Aristotle. They had become dry, narrow, and unfit for the expression of the life of either the pagan or the Christian community. They gradually lost their importance, even the Academy of Plato closing its doors by order of the Emperor Justinian. Intellectual leadership now being in the hands of the Christians, it was up to them to evolve new educational institutions. The chief sources of Christian education were in the catechetical schools operated by the bishops;

the writings and preachings of great teachers like Jerome, Augustine, and Gregory the Great; or, increasingly, the monasteries.

There have been in the West two very different educational traditions. One stresses the needs of order and society and insists that the young are to be taught both the conventional values and morals and the skills useful in performing tasks deemed valuable by society. This was the tradition that dominated the Christian schools, both episcopal and monastic. Conventional Christian values and doctrines were taught unquestionably; and the poets and philosophers were used not for their own sakes, but as treasure-houses from which one extracted passages and sentiments congenial to Christianity and edifying to the spirit. Students were given the skills necessary to train them to fill the needs of society as lawyers, educators, priests, and monks. The other tradition is that which encourages independent thought and original ideas. It concentrates on teaching the young not only the content of a specific subject but also how to think. It is a tradition much more congenial to the prophetic spirit, and like prophecy itself, it has never been popular; for the independent thinker, like the prophet, is often obliged to stand in opposition to the accepted values of society. Socrates was obliged to drink hemlock, and Jesus to carry his cross to Golgotha.

In medieval Christianity, great thinkers like Augustine, Abelard, Bernard, and Aquinas were able to create and develop their own ideas; but on the whole, independence was discouraged. Education conducive to order and social tranquillity prevailed in the medieval, as it had in the ancient, world. The idea of a liberal education involving both breadth and independence of thought was essentially a product of the Renaissance and has since then enjoyed only a tenuous existence.

Toward the end of the fourth century two great fathers of the Church appeared: St. Jerome (c. 347–419) and St. Augustine of Hippo (354–430). Jerome, the son of a well-to-do Dalmatian family, received an education in the classics at Rome and then in the schools of Trier. Although he enjoyed the best prospects for success in the world, he became convinced that the best way to follow Christ was to renounce the world and withdrew to the Syrian desert as a hermit from about 374 to 376. He returned to civilization to finish his education in the great centers of Christian intellectual life at Antioch, Alexandria, and Constantinople. Eventually he went to Rome, where he acquired great influence at the court of Pope Damasus (366–384). Even at Rome, however, Jerome spurned the exercise of worldly power and devoted himself to preaching the virtues of the ascetic and monastic life. This devotion to asceticism, which appears in all his works and letters, was Jerome's chief contribution to developing Christianity: he was probably its strictest moralist since Tertullian. Occasionally his views appear exaggerated, as when he told one recently widowed woman that she ought to mourn the loss of her virginity more than the loss of her spouse. Jerome was also the translator into Latin of the Hebrew Old Testament and the Greek New Testament. This translation became known as the Vulgate (*vulgus,* "the crowd"), from its wide use as the standard Bible of the Middle Ages. Jerome spent the last three decades of his life in withdrawal from the world at a monastery in Bethlehem.

St. Augustine was, after Jesus himself and Paul, the most formative figure in the history of Christian thought and, with Plato and Aristotle, one of the fundamental influences in Western culture as a whole. Philosophy and theology were for six hundred years after Augustine's death largely devoted to the elaboration of his thought.

Augustine was born in 354 in Numidia to a pagan father of the class of *curiales*—citizens with influence and responsibility, whose wealth, however, had been eroded by the oppressive tax policies of the later Roman Empire. His mother, Monica, was a Christian and was later canonized. Like Origen, Augustine early gave evidence of a questing mind, but unlike the Alexandrian, he was not as a youth committed to Christianity. He lived a boy's and young man's life that he later repudiated as sinful. At the age of seventeen he went off to study in the schools of Carthage, where "there sang all around me in my ears a cauldron of unholy loves." There he lived "seduced and seducing, deceived and deceiving, [the prey of] divers lusts."[2] He acquired a mistress, and the following year she bore him a son, whom he named with sincere devotion Adeodatus, "Gift of God." His restless mind led him not only to taverns: "For I bore about a shattered and bleeding soul—yet where to repose it I found not. Not in calm groves, not in games and music, nor in fragrant spots, nor in curious banquetings, nor in the pleasures of the bed and the couch; nor [finally] in books or poesy." He sought all the philosophers and teachers of Carthage—like Justin Martyr trying, and being disappointed by, one philosophy and religion after another.

Augustine's eventual conversion to Christianity was doubtless a product as much of his sense of sin and of the influence of his mother as of purely intellectual considerations. For some years Augustine was an adherent of Manichaeism, a religion with a morbid disgust for the flesh. Founded in the third century by a Mesopotamian named Mani, it was based upon Zoroastrianism with an admixture of Buddhism, Judaism, Christianity, and Gnosticism. Its morality was exceedingly dualistic and strict. Even while embracing this religion, Augustine had many questions and doubts that he could not answer, and he eagerly awaited the arrival in Carthage of Faustus, the most renowned of the Manichaean teachers. When Faustus proved unable to resolve his perplexities, Augustine removed to Italy with his mother, his mistress, and his son, in order there to seek other teachers and other doctrines. For a while he was a Neoplatonist, but in the meantime he had come under the influence of St. Ambrose, who himself had a good knowledge of Greek and understanding of Neoplatonic doctrines.

Ambrose (339–397) is an excellent example of the sociologically interesting generalization that a disproportionately great number of the leaders of the early and medieval Church came from wealthy and influential backgrounds. The son of a wealthy and powerful praetorian prefect, Ambrose himself rose quickly in the

[2]The quotations from the *Confessions* throughout this chapter are from the translation by Edward B. Pusey (New York, 1949).

civil administration. At the time that the bishopric of Milan fell vacant in 374, Ambrose was the civil governor of the province, and his experience, skill, and popularity won him election to the vacant see by acclamation. As bishop, the confidence that sprang of family background and administrative experience permitted Ambrose to exercise considerable influence, not only in the Church but in the State. When the powerful Emperor Theodosius, for example, permitted the massacre of a rebel mob in Thessalonica by his troops, Ambrose excommunicated him and compelled him to do penance and to amend his life.

Under the influence of Ambrose, whose intellectual strengths were as great as his administrative virtues, Augustine began to study seriously the religion his mother had tried to teach him as a child. A certain day while sitting in the garden meditating, Augustine is supposed to have heard the voice of a child at play calling out what sounded to him like "Take up and read!" Receiving this as an omen, he rushed into the house and opened the Bible at random to the passage: " 'Not in rioting and drunkenness, not in chambering and wantonness, not in strife and envying; but put ye on the Lord Jesus Christ.'...No further would I read, nor needed I: for instantly at the end of this sentence, by a light as it were of serenity infused into my heart, all the darkness of doubt vanished away." No more terse description of the experience of conversion is possible. He was shortly baptized. Subsequently he returned to Africa. At Carthage he went into semimonastic retirement with a group of intellectual friends; he took Holy Orders; and he eventually was elected bishop of Hippo, in which post he remained until his death in 430.

The works of Augustine include quantities of sermons, letters, and treatises, like *On Christian Doctrine* and *On the Free Choice of the Will;* but his most justly famous monuments are his *Confessions,* a spiritual autobiography "confessing," i.e., "witnessing to," divine mercy, and his *City of God.* This last was written following the fall of Rome to the Visigoths in 410, in defense against pagan polemicists who argued that Christianity had weakened the empire and prepared the way for its ruin.

It is possible only to sketch some of the most important arguments of this great thinker, who developed and elaborated the thought of St. Paul on such important points as the nature of God, the nature of the world, and the relationship between God and man.

For Augustine the existence of God is unquestionable, not only by virtue of revelation but by the dictates of philosophy. Indeed, to ask whether there is a God is a meaningless question, for God is Being itself. If anything is, God is. Because God is pure Being, he is the "isness" of anything that is: he is perfect Truth, perfect Goodness, and perfect Beauty. All things that are derive their being from God: insofar as they exist at all, they exist with the being of God. Insofar therefore as they are good, they are good with God's goodness; insofar as they are beautiful, they are beautiful with God's beauty; insofar as they are true, they are true with God's truth.

Experience informs us that there are defects in things, and these defects proceed from a lack of Being. Ugliness and evil are not qualities in themselves, but merely the lack of Beauty and Good. Insofar as a tree is ugly, it derives its ugliness not from any positive source, but from the fact that its share of Beauty is deficient. Augustine was thus able to postulate a chain of being, an organization of the universe that was further developed by later theologians, particularly Aquinas, and that has become one of the commonest and most deeply rooted assumptions of Western man. It lent an order to nature similar to the order that was so fervently sought in Christian society.

In the chain of being, at the top stands God, perfect Being, Goodness, Beauty, and Truth. Since matter is subject to change and decay, while spirit is simple and unchanging, God is pure Spirit. Below God in descending order are ranked things according to the degree in which they participate in God's being: according to the degree in which they too are good, beautiful, and spiritual. Of created beings, angels, who are pure spirits, are the highest. Below angels are men (Augustine would have included sentient beings of other planets had he conceived of any). Men are partly matter, but of all material creatures they are the most spiritual. Because they alone of earthly creatures have self-knowledge and a comprehension of good and evil, they have an immortal soul. Below men are the animals in order of their intelligence (for intelligence is equated with spirituality); below animals, vegetables; and below vegetables, inanimate objects. Close to the very bottom of the scale is something that we have never seen and can only conceive of: pure matter, the *hylē* of Aristotle, matter upon which no forms have been impressed. Matter is, as the French philosopher Etienne Gilson puts it, tottering on the verge of unreality. The polar opposite of God is total nonbeing, utter nothingness, complete deprivation and lack of everything, nonexistence. On this scale, things are more good and more real the more spiritual they are; less good and less real the more material they are. This is rooted philosophically in Platonic idealism and is almost the opposite of modern materialism. Augustine would not have been impressed by Doctor Johnson's reply to Bishop Berkeley that if he kicked a stone and it hurt, he knew it was there. Knowledge did not come primarily from sense observation, but, as in the thought of both Socrates and St. Paul, from internal illumination.

In his expression of the chain of being, Augustine created one difficulty that plagued Aquinas later. The chain of being we have just described is purely ontological: it has to do with being. In the ontological sense it is proper to speak of things being "good" to the degree that they partake of Spirit and "evil" insofar as they are deprived of Spirit. But both Augustine and Aquinas confused morality with ontology and tried to interpolate the moral with the ontological scale, claiming that moral evil was also deprivation, lack of Good. But the two scales are not easily conjoined. Ontologically, a man is always "better" than a cow because he is more real, i.e., more spiritual. But we speak of good cows and bad men; further, when we do so, we are usually using "good" and "bad" in different senses. A man is capable of moral evil, and a cow is not. To take another example, an angel is always ontologically better, because more real, than a man. But morally Satan, a fallen angel, is clearly less good than, say, St. Paul. In the moral scale, in fact, Satan would occupy the lowest rank, for Satan is the most morally evil creature in the universe; yet ontologically he is as close as any angel to pure spirituality. This confusion of the moral and the ontological was to haunt moral theology throughout the history of the medieval Church.

To return to Augustine's view of the world: in opposition to the Manichaeism that he had once professed, Augustine denied that the material world was illusory or evil. He agreed with Plato that the world around us was less real than the world of ideas or the world of God, but that it was by no means devoid of reality. Further, since it was created by the good God, it must itself be good. It is impossible to overstate the importance for the history of our civilization of this attitude of Augustine's. His acceptance of the intrinsic value of the world, and therefore of the value of observing it, prevented Christianity from adopting a wholly otherworldly attitude that would have made it impossible for Western science to develop. At the same time, Augustine was extremely important for the development of historical thought. Where most of the Greeks had dismissed time as cyclical and of no inherent importance, Augustine again argued that since God had created time, it must have meaning. If God allowed time to elapse between the Creation and the Redemption, he had some purpose in doing so; God must have been gradually preparing the Jews for the Incarnation. Events in time are therefore real, they move in one direction, and they change through a process of development. It is on these premises that the study of history has proceeded.

For Augustine, then, the study of the world is important. But its importance derives not from itself, but from the fact that it points the way to God who, as absolute Truth and Being, is the natural aim of all our investigations. But how can man, who is limited, comprehend the eternal God? Augustine's answer is that he cannot. The theology of Augustine is essentially analogical. Man calls God "good," but God's goodness is utterly beyond man's comprehension, as are his beauty, his eternity, and all his other qualities. Augustine never lost sight of the true religious experience, the sense of the Wholly Other and therefore wholly unknowable.

Man cannot comprehend God. Yet God would not create an

understanding creature and then deny him all access to truth. We see, therefore, though it is only as through a glass darkly. We examine the things of this world and find in them analogies of God's world. In the beauty of a tree we find the analogy of God's beauty, which is incomprehensibly greater. In the order of the planets we find the analogy of the infinitely greater order of God; from the endurance of the hills we draw the analogy of God's eternity; in the grandeur of mountains we see his tremendous majesty.

Thus the senses have their utility. But there is something other than the external world that we can examine, something which is a better analogy of God than anything we can see: our own minds. In our intellectual ascent to God, we mount one step higher and meditate upon our consciousness, which of all things on earth is the thing most directly formed in the image of God. Like Socrates and Plato, Augustine affirmed that the truest knowledge comes from internal illumination, for it is within us that the Holy Spirit dwells. As Augustine's acceptance of the world encouraged science, so his emphasis upon the light within greatly encouraged the development of Christian mysticism; for the final step in self-understanding is the complete opening up of the soul, so that, as Paul had said, I live no longer, but Christ within me. At the apex of Augustine's intellectual order was, again, the spirit of prophecy.

Augustine's view of man's relationship to God was based upon the Pauline notion of sin and grace. God in his goodness had created man with the potentiality for moral goodness. But moral goodness requires free choice, and so God gave man absolute freedom to choose to obey God or to follow his own selfish will. Adam and Eve, who represented all mankind, made the choice: they disobeyed God. The picking of the forbidden fruit is a symbol of this disobedience. In his *Confessions,* Augustine used a similar incident in his own life to illustrate the nature of sin. While playing as a boy with some friends, he helped them steal pears from an orchard. The stealing of a pear is to the secular mind not such a great crime, but for Augustine the important thing is the disposition of the conscience. He knew that God wished him not to pick the pear; but in order to appear a good fellow to his companions, he picked it anyway. The essence of sin is comprehended in this act: to say to God, "Not thy will, O Lord, but mine, be done."

The original sin of Adam and Eve had enormous consequences. Not only was man expelled from Paradise, but he bore in his very nature the mark of his sin. Adam was wholly free to choose good or evil, but having made his choice, his nature was then inclined to sin. Adam ("the Man") represents the entire human race, so that every baby is born with this inclination. All mankind is afflicted, therefore, not only with the punishment but also with the guilt accruing to sin.

Augustine went further, and argued that since the Fall we have been not only inclined but actually bound to sin. We made our choice in Adam, and we are therefore inherently corrupt. There is nothing whatever that man can do to save himself from sin or to storm the gates of Paradise.

In strict justice, God is obliged to do nothing for us. He made a contract with Adam that Adam should be happy as long as he obeyed God; since Adam did not fulfill his obligations, the contract is consequently void. Hell is separation from God, and it is not God who has condemned man but man who has damned himself. Yet God is not only just but merciful, and he wills to redeem us. He gives us a second chance. Since man cannot save himself, it is incumbent upon God to save him. This is the meaning of the Incarnation: God becomes man and dies for man in order to redeem him from his guilt. The Passion of Christ opens again the road to Paradise that man has blocked. As the Old Adam ("the Man") represented all men in their guilt, so Christ, who was also called "the Man" or "the New Adam," represents all men in their redemption. We are part of the mystical body of Adam, and we are part of the Mystical Body of Christ.

If Christ's redemptive act was cosmic in significance, what can the individual do to participate in his own salvation? Through his own most grievous fault in Adam, the individual is born damned and incapable of saving himself. There is literally absolutely nothing a man can do to free himself from sin, for there is nothing good in a man save that which comes from God. All he can do is open his heart and await the gift of grace, of God's life. Grace generates faith, and a man heretofore spiritually dead becomes alive with God's life. The simplest analogy is to a radio set, which, silent until plugged into the circuit, comes to life when filled with electrical energy.

In the course of his meditations on grace and salvation, Augustine touched upon two of the most perennially difficult questions of Christian theology. The first is the problem of evil: if God is both good and omnipotent, how can there be evil in the world? The partial answer, Augustine suggests, is that the moral evil in the world comes from sinful man (or angels), not from God. God tolerates this evil because it is the necessary consequence of a truly free will: if God had *obliged* Adam not to sin, Adam would have had no free choice, and without free choice there can be no virtue. God tolerates vice because its existence is necessary to that of virtue.

A second partial answer is that the ontological evil in the world, i.e., the lack of perfect Goodness, is the necessary consequence of a created universe. God creates the universe from nothing; the universe is consequently other than God and lacking in perfection. The variety in the world means that of necessity some things lack perfection more than others. Again, the existence of imperfection is the logical consequence of the existence of anything at all. To blame God for putting imperfections in the universe is precisely like blaming the cheesemaker for putting holes in a Swiss cheese. The holes are necessary for the existence of a cheese that is Swiss; and in an ontological sense the holes do not exist at all: they are merely cheeselessness. So the imperfections of the universe are necessary. Ontologically, they do not really exist: they are simple deprivation and lack.

The other perennial problem is that of predestination. It has always been difficult to reconcile the freedom of man with the omnipotence of God, though philosophically it can be done and has been done.[3] Augustine left them unreconciled. He accepted the Christian doctrine of free will, but his theology leaves it little room;

---

[3]By Boethius and Molina, among others.

and he strongly condemned the British theologian Pelagius for teaching that a man might without grace form his own will to goodness and by means of a good life save himself. At most, Augustine argued, free will is brought into play in man's response to grace: "We conclude that a man is not justified by the precepts of a holy life but by faith in Jesus Christ. That is to say, not by the law of works, but by that of faith; not by the letter, but by the spirit; not by the merits of deeds, but by gratuitous grace."[4]

Augustine was in fact inclined to the even stricter position that the power of God's grace was such that no one could refuse it. Yet are we then all saved? Is God's life given to us all? No, Augustine answered, reluctantly but firmly. Remember that in strict justice God is obliged to save no one. It would be a great mercy if he saved only one among millions. Remember too that God damns no one; we have in Adam condemned ourselves. In his great mercy, God chooses those whom he wishes to save; he simply leaves others to their own just damnation. Many have found this doctrine of predestination and grace faulty in its apparent limitation of God's mercy as well as of man's freedom, and through the centuries there have been both dissent and modifications. Yet predestination remains, in one form or another, the most common teaching of the Catholic Church[5] as well as of those Churches influenced by Luther and Calvin, who chose Augustine as their chief inspiration after the Bible. Bishop, monk, philosopher, and moralist, source of both Catholic and Protestant theology, Augustine died in 430 with his eyes fixed upon the penitential psalms while the Vandals were at the gates of his episcopal city of Hippo.

The monasteries, as well as great individual teachers, were a source of Christian education. Monasticism was founded in the

[4]*On the Spirit and the Letter,* xiii, 22, in Erich Przywara, *Augustine Synthesis* (New York, 1958), p. 316.
[5]See Father Garrigou-Lagrange, *Predestination* (London, 1953).

spirit of prophecy, and the monasteries came to be the most common homes for ascetics and mystics wishing to pursue an individual and prophetic road to God. But like the Church as a whole, the monasteries came gradually to be both more ordered internally and more of a force for order in society.

In the beginning, the rules and regulations of monasticism varied greatly from community to community, but by the end of the sixth century a few were becoming general and common. Of these the most important were the Rule of St. Columban, followed by the numerous and influential monasteries founded by Irish missionaries, and the Rule of St. Benedict. That of St. Benedict gradually prevailed, and in the eighth and ninth centuries it was adopted by the Frankish kings as the official rule for all monasteries in their domains. By establishing one monastic order, the Benedictine, the rulers of Church and State checked dissensions and disparities within monasticism and turned it into an organized force for social order.

St. Benedict was born about 480 in the small town of Nursia in the Sabine hills near Rome. Like many monastic leaders, he sprang from a noble and wealthy family. He studied for a short while at Rome and then, renouncing the world, became a monk, eventually founding the abbey of Monte Cassino. There about 540 he established his "Rule"—his book of monastic regulations. For St. Benedict, the purpose of the monastery was to provide an environment where men might meditate away from the cares and distractions of this world. Some of the monks were priests; others were lay brothers. Monasticism was a fulfillment of the teachings of Christ and Paul to put away the world and to fill oneself wholly with Christ. Each monk had to vow poverty, chastity, and obedience to his ecclesiastical superiors, thereby suppressing the three greatest temptations: money, sex, and ambition. The chief duty of the monk was prayer. Benedict ordered that eight times in the twenty-four-hour day the monks would meet in the chapel to recite the community prayers called the Office. Throughout the rest of the day, they were to offer up privately not only their words and thoughts but also their other duties and labors as prayers to God. The monks were to live very simply and to do all their own work: carpentry, gardening, cooking, weaving, and the rest. A small portion of the day was set aside for sacred study, but the monasteries were not at first centers of intellectual endeavor. Classical learning was still feared as being pagan and corrupt: both monasticism and Christianity itself needed to be more firmly established before they could approach the classics with tolerance, much less enthusiasm.

The central purpose of monasticism was prayer, and this was conceived as a public duty. The monks prayed for the welfare of the entire world and believed that in so doing they were performing a social function more important than any other. The monastic life was not an escape from responsibility to one's fellow men.

Indeed, the monasteries came to fulfill social needs in other ways as well. From the fifth to the tenth century, when Europe was beset by internal dissensions and decay and by frequent barbarian assaults from without, the civil and ecclesiastical structure of authority was badly weakened. In this situation the monasteries (though they, too, were subject to barbarian attack) stood as islands of relative tranquillity and order. In the midst of economic decline and the reversion of land to waste, the monks cleared and tilled and rendered fields productive. In time of famine they fed the poor. They provided the only care for the sick available in most areas. They cared for penniless widows and orphans and provided shelter for those who traveled on the unsafe highways. And in the seventh and eighth centuries they became centers of education and learning.

Though Benedict himself had allowed little time for study, other monastic leaders encouraged it more. Cassiodorus, a scholar of sixth-century Italy, founded a monastery in which the chief duty of the monks, after prayer, was to study, to copy manuscripts, to write, and to teach. Cassiodorus and his contemporary Boethius, who was not himself a monk, evolved a curriculum based upon that of the classical schools, which became the basis of education throughout the Middle Ages. This consisted of the "seven liberal arts": grammar, rhetoric, dialectic, arithmetic, astronomy, geometry, and music. The Benedictines themselves gradually devoted a larger proportion of their day to teaching. This was not only owing to the inclination of the monks but also to the needs of society, for after the classical schools were closed, the monasteries became the chief centers of learning.

There were usually two schools in each monastery, the "inner school," in which were trained the boys who were destined to be monks, and the "outer school," where the others were taught. Though the laity was never wholly illiterate, most of the boys even in the outer school were planning to be priests, and it was this trained clergy to which the administration of both the Church and the State was usually consigned.

The monks also labored in the *scriptoria,* where they copied manuscripts, the only way of reproducing books before the invention of printing. They copied not only Christian books but also the pagan classics, and we would possess nothing but a few fragments of the classical writers were it not for their labors. In the scriptoria those monks who were so inclined could also exercise their creative urge. Many of their manuscripts are beautifully illuminated, and these illustrations constitute the largest artistic genre of the early Middle Ages. The monasteries also produced original works of theology, saints' lives, chronicles, and even drama.

The monasteries were the most important cultural force of the early Middle Ages, not only in the formation of Christian order and culture within the boundaries of the old Roman Empire, but in the extension of the benefits of Christianity to previously pagan countries. The monks, particularly from Ireland and England, were the most vigorous and effective missionaries since apostolic times.

Thus in the period from the fourth to the seventh century the peace of the Church, the growth of Christian institutions, and the spread of the Christian religion prepared the way for the establishment of a Western Christian order in the eighth century.

The Formation of the Medieval Order, 700–900

In the eighth century the lines of the Western civilization that was emerging out of the classical world were beginning to be discernible. The Mediterranean area, which had been the center of the commercial, administrative, and intellectual life of the Roman Empire, was now split into three distinct parts: the West, Byzantium, and Islam. Out of Arabia in the seventh century had come the warriors of Islam, a new religion based in part upon Judaism and Christianity but transformed by the teachings of the Prophet Mohammed, who claimed to be the successor of Moses and Jesus and to offer a fuller revelation than theirs. Islam advanced with phenomenal rapidity, conquering Persia and thrusting eastward into India and central Asia. Westward, the Moslems seized Syria and Palestine from the Roman Empire and then moved rapidly to conquer all of North Africa as far as the Atlantic and the Straits of Gibraltar. By 700, Islam had deprived Christianity of its wealthiest regions, its most intellectually prominent cities, and its most venerable shrines. Syria, Egypt, Alexandria, Carthage, Jerusalem, all fell into the hands of the Prophet's followers, who in 673–678 and again in 717–718 laid siege to Constantinople itself.

The Christian East and the Christian West were themselves

drawing apart. Since the death of Justinian in 565, the political authority of Constantinople in the West had slowly declined. Owing to the general decline in population and commerce in the Mediterranean world since the third century, the economic contacts between the two regions also grew more tenuous. Intellectually, the gap was especially wide. Greek had always remained the cultural and commercial language of the East, but Latin had been widely used for centuries in administration and law. It had even made some progress as a language of culture, and in the sixth century, for example, there were more chairs of Latin than of Greek literature at the higher school of Constantinople. Gradually, in the course of the seventh and eighth centuries, as the unity of the empire faded, the use of Latin also declined, and Greek reasserted itself in the East in every area of life.

The policies of the Emperor Leo the Isaurian (717–741) widened the gap between East and West. Leo reinstalled Greek as the sole language of law and administration; he reorganized his army and administration in an efficient and autocratic fashion; and he adopted and tried to enforce a religious doctrine, Iconoclasm, which was repugnant to the popes and to the people of the West as a whole. The papal resistance to the emperor's Iconoclastic edicts ordering the destruction of all statues and pictures in churches was very popular in the West and was a major step in the ecclesiastical separation of East and West, a separation that was already visible in the liturgy and practices of the two Churches. Greek was the language of the Eastern Mass, Latin that of the Western; and while worship throughout most of the West was according to the rite practiced at Rome, the East used wholly different forms. The date of Easter came to differ. Married men might be priests in the East; but the Western Church took increasing pains to enforce the celibacy of the clergy. By the eighth century the papacy had adopted the doctrine of the double procession.[1] Of

---

[1]This was the notion that the Holy Spirit proceeds from both the Father and the Son. The Greeks usually preferred the single procession from the Father and objected to the Western insertion of the *Filioque* ("and from the Son") clause into the Nicene Creed.

most practical importance, the patriarchs of Rome and Constantinople continued to argue over precedence and to dispute the jurisdiction of territories. By the eighth century, the divisions had become so great that from then on it is more proper to speak of a Byzantine rather than an Eastern Roman Empire.

While the East grew more Greek, the West was moving toward a new cultural synthesis. To Christian culture, already a synthesis of Jewish, Greek, and Roman elements, were now added Celtic and Teutonic influences derived from the Germanic invaders and Celtic missionaries. By the eighth century, western Europe had a cultural identity that set it clearly apart from both Islam and Byzantium.

It was gaining a political identity as well. The unity of the empire had technically never been breached, and the barbarian kings often took Roman titles like that of consul and professed themselves subject to the emperor at Constantinople. In practice, however, the new kingdoms were quite independent. In 700, there were four major political entities in the West: the Visigothic kingdom in Spain, the Anglo-Saxon kingdoms in Britain, the Frankish kingdom in Gaul and Germany, and the Lombard kingdom in Italy. In addition, the Byzantine Empire retained footholds in Italy in the regions of Rome and Ravenna.

In the course of the eighth century, two of these four entities were removed by conquest: in 711–713 Spain fell to Islam, and by 774 the Franks had annexed Lombard Italy. Scandinavia, the Slavic countries, and vast tracts of Germany were yet to be converted and civilized, and the Anglo-Saxon kingdoms were small, divided, and isolated. This left the Frankish kingdom as the logical center for the formation of a Christian order in the West. The Franks had been pagans at the time of their irruption into the empire at the beginning of the fifth century, but by the end of that century they had been converted to Roman Catholicism.

65

This made them naturally more favorable to the papacy than had been the Ostrogoths, Visigoths, or Vandals, who were all Arian heretics. An alliance of the political power of the Franks with the religious power of the papacy came in the course of the eighth century to provide the focus of unity for Western civilization and the basis for the construction of a Christian society.

Franks and papacy were alike incalculably aided in this endeavor by the activity of Irish and Anglo-Saxon missionaries. The eighth-century synthesis was, curiously, less the result of a reaching out for power from the center than a centripetal movement by the people on the peripheries of Western culture. Of the popes, for example, only Gregory the Great had taken the initiative in launching a great missionary effort: the sending of St. Augustine of Canterbury to England in 595–597. The Gauls also did missionary work, but the greatest numbers with the greatest enthusiasm came from Ireland and England.

Ireland, which had never been part of the Roman Empire, was pagan until the mid-fifth century. The ancient legend is that St. Patrick came to convert the island in 432. Neither the date nor the personality of Patrick are at all well established, but it is clear that Christianity had taken root among the Irish by the beginning of the sixth century. Patrick probably came to Ireland from Lérins, a strict monastery in southern Gaul, and the Christianity he imported was very ascetic and monastic in spirit. Particularly after the conquest of Christian Britain by the pagan Anglo-Saxons, Ireland was to some extent isolated from the Continental Church, and Irish Catholicism adopted certain peculiar characteristics. Some of these peculiarities were minor, though they exercised theologians at the time considerably: the Irish celebrated Easter on a different date each year from the Romans, and Irish monks wore a different kind of tonsure. More significant was the role of monasticism in Ireland. The Irish Church was the only one in Christendom to be dominated completely by monasticism, not only morally but even administratively. In Ireland the dioceses were centered not around towns (of which there were few), but around monasteries, and the abbot of the chief monastery of the diocese filled the function of bishop. Thus from the beginning Irish Catholicism has had the ascetic coloration that has continued to distinguish it down to the present.

Most important for the development of the Church as a whole was the Irish emphasis upon the Christian concept of life as a *peregrinatio,* literally, "pilgrimage." One of the basic assumptions of medieval Christianity was that man's life in this world was merely a *peregrinatio,* a wandering through a valley of sorrows until he reaches his true native land in God. The Irish monks took this idea literally and determined to imitate the apostles by going forth and preaching the Gospel to all nations. Before Gregory sent Augustine to carry Roman Christianity to the English, Irish missionaries like the sixth-century St. Colum Cille (Columba) and the seventh-century Sts. Chad and Aidan had converted what is now southern Scotland and northern England to Celtic Christianity. The English kingdom of Northumbria went on to become one of the great centers of Celtic culture, which from the sixth to the eighth centuries was one of the most brilliant in Europe for the originality of its poetry and painting, for the quantity and quality of its manuscripts, and for the erudition of its theologians. Nor did the Irish stop at Britain. St. Columbanus (fl. 600) and his followers founded monasteries in Gaul and in Italy, preaching the Gospel, establishing schools, and elevating moral and intellectual standards.

By 650, in a process well described by the great English historian St. Bede, the Roman and Irish Catholics in Britain were at loggerheads owing to the divergence of their practices. With the intolerance of an age in which nice points of theology appeared very important, neither side wished to compromise. Accordingly, in 663 or 664 King Oswy of Northumbria called a great synod at the monastery of Whitby. There the Irish monk St. Colman debated the virtues of Celtic Christianity against the English abbot Wilfred of Ripon, later bishop of York. After the arguments were concluded, the king decided in favor of Rome, declaring that he could find in Scripture arguments for the primacy of Peter but none for that of Ireland. Colman and the Irish packed up and returned sadly home, and by the end of the century most of Ireland had itself accepted the Roman customs. But Celtic Christianity had not been wholly defeated, for it made lasting contributions to the synthesis of the European Church. It was the Irish, for example, who introduced private penance and secret confession, as against the old custom of public confession and penance. Meticulously, the Irish invented "penitentials," books describing in detail all sins with the appropriate penance attached to each. Nor did they slacken their missionary efforts after their absorption by Rome; throughout the Middle Ages they were found as far east as Warsaw and Kiev; there were Irish bishops in Austria and southern Italy, Irish monasteries all over Europe, and Irish scholars at the great schools and courts.

Meanwhile, the English combined a close devotion to the Roman Church with a missionary fervor derived from the Irish; and throughout most of the Middle Ages the papacy had no more loyal supporters than the English kings and people, who paid the popes a yearly voluntary tribute called "Peter's pence." The English, Teutonic in blood, Roman in religion, and strongly influenced by the Celts, were the perfect vehicle for European synthesis; and English missionaries helped to cement Christian society by bringing the papacy and the Franks together.

The first of the English missionaries to the Continent was the victor of Whitby, St. Wilfred of York. Wilfred's mission began rather by accident: he was a politically inclined prelate with many enemies, and it was in the course of a mission to Rome in order to plead his case against his opponents that in 678 he found himself in Frisia (the present Netherlands). Learning that the Frisians were pagans, he preached to them awhile during the winter of that year. Returning home, he spread the word that there was need for missionary work just across the North Sea. St. Willibrord, St. Boniface (Winfrith), and many others answered his call, and for a century there was as great an outpouring of English missionaries as there had been of Irish. In Charlemagne's time, a Frankish monk complained that the English swarmed through Gaul as thick as bees.

The most important, and certainly the most energetic, English missionary was St. Boniface (c. 680–755). Trained in a monastery from the age of five, Boniface absorbed both learning and zeal. He had built a reputation both as a scholar and an administrator when, nearly forty years old, he determined to follow the example of Willibrord and undertake a mission to the Frisians, whose paganism had proved violent and resistant to conversion. In 716 he arrived on the Continent and spent much of the spring and summer in Frisia. After initial difficulties, he realized that his work would have much greater chance of success if he could enlist the assistance of the two most prestigious men in western Europe: the chief minister of the Franks and the pope.

The Merovingian kings of the Franks had gradually lost their power by delegating it to the "mayor of the palace" or chief minister. At the time, the chief minister was Charles Martel (714–741), the future victor of Tours and grandfather of Charlemagne. Boniface applied to Charles for help, and both Charles and later his son Pepin the Short (741–768) supported the mission of Boniface, from political need as well as Christian duty. It was to their advantage to convert the neighboring savage pagans and so secure their borders, to improve the organization of the Church and so enhance public order, and to raise the intellectual level of the clergy so as to obtain more qualified administrators. If English missionaries were willing and able to help achieve these ends, the Frankish leaders could only assent with right good Christian will. Continuing his journey to Rome in 718, Boniface also enlisted the support of Pope Gregory II and his successors, who welcomed the work of the English in converting the pagans and building a well-organized transalpine Church with a strong sense of the prestige of the see of Peter. After preaching for three years in Thuringia and Hesse, he returned to Rome, where he was consecrated missionary bishop.

Boniface and his followers labored mightily throughout Gaul and Germany, founding monasteries and schools, preaching to the pagans, organizing ecclesiastical administration, and encouraging order and obedience to the pope and to the chief minister of the Franks. Boniface's mission was one of the most important episodes in European history, for it quickened a spirit of reform and renewal that would time and again reappear until it finally culminated in the papal revolution of the eleventh century. A tireless preacher, Boniface set in motion a spirit of moral reform that was implemented by episcopal synods and by the capitularies (ordinances or administrative edicts) of the Frankish rulers. The monasteries he founded became centers not only of moral but also of intellectual advance; and, with the encouragement of the Frankish rulers, this cultural progress was accelerated at the time of Charlemagne. Boniface and his fellow workers greatly advanced the conversion of Germany to Christianity, thus laying the foundations of medieval German culture. They founded and organized dioceses, Boniface himself being named archbishop of Mainz with a certain preeminence among the bishops of Germany.

The labors of Boniface worked in every way toward the formation of the new European synthesis. A somewhat intolerant as well as fervent man, he directed his saintly displeasure against illiterate priests who celebrated Mass badly, against ignorant peasants whose Christianity was still colored by pagan superstitions, and against heretics. He even combated the Irish monks and missionaries because their conformity to the practices of the Roman Church was still imperfect, and he sought with much success to replace them in positions of influence by men more loyal to the pope. The transalpine hierarchy, heretofore virtually independent, was brought gradually into dependence upon Rome.

The hierarchy was beginning to take the general form that it would have until the papal revolution of the eleventh century. It was still usual for the priests of a diocese to live in the city with the bishop and to serve the countryside on circuit tours. But the parish, rural or urban, became increasingly common from the eighth century on. The parishes, which were the smallest administrative units of the Church, were each headed by a priest who was responsible to the bishop of the diocese but lived in his parish. Dioceses in turn were grouped into provinces, and though the old office of metropolitan had lapsed, its place was taken by that of archbishop. The archbishop's authority over the other bishops of his province was tenuous, but he at least had the right to call provincial synods. Sometimes the most important archbishop in a country would have the often merely honorary title of primate. In England, the archbishop of Canterbury was the primate; in Germany the primacy was disputed between Mainz and Cologne, and in France between Lyon, Sens, and Reims. In Italy, of course, there was no rival to Rome. All these were responsible to the pope to a degree that varied in proportion to their own strength compared with that of the papacy.

More than anyone between Gregory the Great and Charlemagne, Boniface advanced the cause of Christian unity and order. The energetic, indeed sometimes officious, saint was murdered in 755 by a band of robbers in Frisia, where he had returned at the advanced age of nearly eighty in a final effort to complete the conversion of that stubborn people.

The labors of the English missionaries were accomplished with only the moral support of the popes, who gave them honors and advice but very little practical aid. Yet in other respects the eighth-century popes were not only vigorous but almost revolutionary. To be one of the foundation stones of European order, the papacy needed three things: independence from interference by the imperial government in Constantinople, the establishment of an independent base of power in central Italy, and an alliance with an important Western power. These aims were accomplished by a succession of four extremely able popes: Gregory II (715–731), Gregory III (731–741), Zachary (741–752), and Stephen III (752–757).

On the accession of Gregory II in 715, the position of the papacy was insecure in the extreme. Byzantine power was still considerable in Italy, and during the seventh century few popes had dared to resist the imperial will. One who did, Martin I (649–655), was summarily arrested and sent into exile. Early in the eighth century the Emperor Leo the Isaurian established a military officer at Ravenna with the title of exarch and the duty of imposing military and civil order in the peninsula. The pope himself was still considered an imperial administrator, responsible for the military as well as the civil affairs of Rome and its environs. The exarch, acting for the emperor, levied troops throughout Italy and imposed heavy taxes, which he sent to Constantinople. These impositions galled the Italian population, especially because the emperor seemed very little interested in using them to defend the West. Preoccupied with the massive Arab threat from the east, Leo the Isaurian and his successors used the money they collected in Italy for the defense of Constantinople and Asia Minor. Italy itself was left open to the inroads of the Lombards. By 715 these hostile and still largely savage people had conquered most of the interior of the Italian peninsula, and their announced aim was the occupation of both Ravenna and Rome.

The popes were in an untenable position. They were obliged to resist the Lombards, but they found themselves hindered, not helped, by their connections with the emperor. The issuing of the decree on Iconoclasm by Leo the Isaurian in 726 was the last straw. Gregory II not only refused to publish the decree, but also seized the opportunity to stop sending tax money or troops to the emperor or the exarch. The exarch threatened to march against him, and there was an unsuccessful plot against the pope's life, but Gregory had taken a long step toward independence.

At the same time, Gregory made other efforts to improve the

position of the papacy. It was he who gave the initial encouragement to St. Boniface, a policy whose rewards, though somewhat delayed, were to be rich. The prestige of the see of Peter, already great, was enhanced, and many from northern Europe began to make pilgrimages to Rome.

Gregory made concerted efforts to build the temporal influence of the popes. This influence rested upon two bases, the first of which was the powers they exercised as Byzantine administrators, powers they appropriated as their own as the emperor grew weaker. Also, the pope was the possessor of the "patrimony of St. Peter," land bequeathed or given to the successors of the Prince of the Apostles by pious donors. This land, much of it rich and fertile and populated by serfs, yielded a steady source of income. Gregory II began to wed administrative to proprietary strength, a policy that helped eventually to establish the "papal states" as a viable political entity.

Politically, however, the position of the papacy was still precarious. They played the Byzantines against the Lombards and the Lombards against the Byzantines, with the contradictory hopes that neither side would win and that peace and tranquillity would be restored to Italy. It became clear that a third power must be invited to eliminate both sides. This could mean only one thing: the Franks. Spain was in the hands of the Moslems; the English kingdoms were distant and disunited. Only the Franks were nearby, Christian, and powerful. When the Lombard king, Liutprand, temporarily took Ravenna in 732, it looked as if the balance of power were finally going to be irremediably upset. Liutprand announced his intention of taking possession of Rome, and in 739 Gregory II's successor, Gregory III, accordingly appealed to Charles Martel. The Frankish minister, however, was indebted to the Lombard king, who had helped him clear southern Gaul of the Moslems, and he refused to help. Pope Zachary was able to establish an uneasy truce with the Lombards, but the final fall of Ravenna and the exarchate to the new Lombard king, Aistulf, in 751 set off a new crisis.

The popes continued to lay up Frankish support against their troubles. In 750, Charles Martel's son Pepin decided to become king in name as he already was in power, and he deposed the last weak representative of the Merovingian dynasty. For these proceedings he asked the approval of Pope Zachary, who was delighted to concur and thereby to place the Franks in his debt.

Zachary's successor Stephen II (III) did not hesitate to submit the bill for services rendered. While Aistulf was threatening Rome, Stephen undertook the first recorded papal journey north of the Alps, meeting Pepin at Ponthion in southern Gaul in January, 754. He remained during the rest of the winter in Gaul, where he confirmed Pepin's royal dignity and consecration, granting him the further title of "Roman patrician." In return he secured Pepin's promise to invade Italy and to restore to the pope the lands overrun by the Lombards.

The events of 750–754 did much to enhance the alliance of the papacy and the Franks, but they also foreshadowed future conflict. For the time being, the interests of the two parties coincided: to defeat the Lombards and the Byzantines, to remove the influence of Constantinople from the West, and to create a viable Christian order in Western society. But each party cherished its own particular view of the way in which that order was to be constructed. When Pepin was crowned by the Frankish bishops in 751, he was anointed with holy oil. The ceremony was deliberately and directly copied from the coronation of Solomon in the Book of Kings. The implication was that Pepin, like David and Solomon, ruled as the chosen one of the Lord and that, like the kings over Israel, he had a certain spiritual authority over the people of God, an authority that amounted to semi-priestly powers. In the actual conduct of ecclesiastical affairs, Pepin made it clear that, great though his respect for the pope and the authority of St. Peter might be, it was the king who had the duty to provide for the welfare of the Church in his own domain, to call synods, to regulate the monasteries, and to issue administrative edicts concerning ecclesiastical order. The consecration of Pepin wrapped this practical power in a theoretical package. The precedents for royal control of the Western Church were established.

At the same time, the popes were busily enhancing their own power and prestige. Gregory II and his successors had taken care to build up the papal patrimony, but the weakness of their political situation never escaped their attention. It occurred to someone at the papal court, probably around 750 (although some historians place the date as much as sixty years later), that it was possible to exalt papal power immeasurably simply by producing a certain document. There was an old legend that Pope St. Sylvester had cured Constantine the Great of leprosy and that in return Constantine had granted him great dignities and wide lands. If only that document were now to be produced, the unknown papalists reflected, how much benefit might accrue! The only difficulty was that the document was missing from the papal archives. It was missing because it had never existed, the whole story being fictional; but the papal advisers supposed that it had merely been lost and undertook to supply the deficiency with their own pens. The result was the "Donation of Constantine," a fantastic document in which Constantine conferred upon Sylvester his crown, his insignia, and all his imperial dignities. These Sylvester modestly returned, but the impression was left that the emperor owed his powers to papal generosity. In addition, Constantine gave the pope wide lands throughout the empire. It was possible to interpret part of the document as a grant of the entire Western empire to the popes: "We give to...Sylvester, the Universal Pope...the city of Rome and all the provinces, districts, and cities of Italy and the Western regions...."[2]

These papalist ideas seem to have had wide currency. When Pepin met Stephen III at Ponthion, the king's son, the future Charlemagne, saw his father dismount from his horse and perform ceremonially the function of a groom for the pope. And in 755, when Pepin fulfilled his promises and defeated the Lombards, wresting away many of the territories they had conquered from the Byzantines, the king received two embassies. One was from

[2]In Sidney Z. Ehler and John B. Morrall, trans. and eds., *Church and State through the Centuries* (Westminster, Md., 1954), pp. 16–22.

the emperor, thanking Pepin for his efforts and requesting the return of the conquered territories. The other was from the pope, adjuring him to "hasten to restore to St. Peter what, under your hand and seal, you promised for the good of your soul." It was to the pope rather than to the Eastern emperor that the ruler of the Franks gave the disputed lands, in a "Donation of Pepin" that was confirmed by treaty in 756. The popes were now the temporal rulers of a strip stretching completely across the Italian peninsula from Rome to Ravenna.

These proceedings did much to widen the breach between the East and the West, a breach illustrated by documents and coins: until the eighth century, Rome had used Byzantine coinage, but beginning with Gregory III the popes issued their own coins. Until 772, the popes dated their documents by the regnal year of the emperor at Constantinople; from 772 to 802, by their own regnal year; and after 802, by the regnal year of the king of the Franks as new emperor in the West. An enormous revolution had been effected: the papacy had extricated itself from dependence upon Constantinople and thereby made itself one of the foci for the emerging order of Western Christianity. In the process the popes had greatly enhanced their theoretical position, their prestige north of the Alps, and their temporal power in Italy.

But for everything there is a price. The price was the growing dependence of the papacy upon the king of the Franks, who emerged as the other focus of Western order. Relieved of the pressures of Byzantines and Lombards, the popes had now to struggle to retain their prestige and freedom of action within the powerful Frankish embrace. Though Pepin might have held the bridle of Stephen's horse at Ponthion, it was Pepin's armies upon whom the pope relied for protection; and from that moment on, the welfare of the papacy was firmly bound to the welfare of the Frankish state.

But this explicit dependence was only the most obvious, not the most serious, of the disadvantages of the new situation. The Constantinian Peace of the Church had been recreated in the West. The papacy became one of the two great pillars of society. The popes became temporal as well as spiritual rulers, with a material stake in the social order. The Church increased its power in order that it might mold society according to the principles of Christian order. But society supported the Church to the extent that it seemed socially useful. The goals of Christianity came to be confused with those of secular society. A *societas christiana* was established in the West, and the Church, forgetful of its prophetic duty of judging society, became its servant. Religiosity, the defense of the status quo, replaced religion. The new order was necessary, but it was also necessarily a failure.

The greatest and most successful proponent of the new Christian society was Charlemagne, Charles the Great, who restored the imperial title to the West. The *regnum Francorum* (kingdom of the Franks) was miraculously transformed into something called by Charlemagne's advisers the *imperium christianum.* Charlemagne completed the formation of the European synthesis that earlier in the century had been promoted by the labors of Boniface. His empire came to include almost the entire West, to unite the cultures of Latin, Teuton, and Celt, to enhance moral and intellectual order, and to knit Church and State together into one new order of society.

On the death of Pepin in 768, Charlemagne and his brother Carloman were both heirs to his powers; but in 771, when Carloman retired voluntarily to a monastery, Charlemagne was left sole ruler. In 773, threatened by a revival of Lombard power, Pope Hadrian II issued an appeal to Charlemagne, who descended into Italy and captured the Lombard capital at Pavia. He thereupon assumed the Lombard crown and declared the Lombard kingdom annexed to that of the Franks. To the pope he confirmed a "Donation of Charlemagne," but he soon made it clear that the pope was supposed to rule in Italy as a representative of the Frankish crown. In the context of Charlemagne's whole policy, the conquest of

Italy is one of a number of wars he fought to secure his borders. He completed the pacification and conversion of Germany, for example, by a series of bloody campaigns against the Saxons. But the annexation of Italy had the further effect of consummating the alliance between the papacy and the Franks: the pope was now a Frankish, as he had formerly been a Byzantine, official.

Charlemagne made it abundantly clear that he believed that his anointing as king consecrated him to rule the Church as well as the State. He could not have believed otherwise, since no one in the Middle Ages believed it was possible, let alone desirable, to separate the two. Religion and the State were together the public expression of the life of society. For Charlemagne, an orderly Church was part of the general public order, and he was responsible for its direction, with the help of the pope and the other bishops.

Having embraced the idea of a Christian society, the Church was obliged to serve the purposes of society. In practical terms, control of the Church by the king was politically necessary. The Church was one of the few institutions powerful enough to be an effective force for order. Accordingly Charlemagne used clergymen in his administration. He employed bishops as his representatives in the provinces and invested them with military as well as civil authority. Bishops like those of Reims and Cologne came to have as much political power and influence as the greatest feudal lords among the laity. Bishops and lay lords were sent out by the central government as *missi dominici* to see that local administrators were properly fulfilling their duties. The king, relying heavily as he did upon the support of the bishops, had to make sure that they were men he could trust, so he reserved the right to approve all episcopal elections and on occasion to depose refractory clerics. The Frankish assemblies issued capitularies dealing with ecclesiastical and civil problems alike.

Considering himself responsible for the intellectual and moral welfare of society, Charlemagne ordered the bishops to call reform synods and to enforce their decrees. He founded a system of education, with its center at his own palace school, to which he attracted great scholars from all over Europe, and he issued orders that each bishop should conduct a school in his diocese. Thus he took under the royal wing the reform movements begun by Boniface. This had the double effect of advancing moral and intellectual reform while bringing the Church into greater dependence upon the State. So true was this that Charlemagne, like Constantine, did not hesitate in summoning councils to deal with matters of doctrine and in ordering his advisers to make theological pronouncements on his behalf. At the synod of Frankfurt in 794, for example, he condemned a Spanish heresy called Adoptionism,[3] while his chief adviser, Alcuin, and others wrote tracts modifying the decisions of the ecumenical council of II Nicaea (787) in regard to Iconoclasm. This council outlawed Iconoclasm and thus brought the East back into closer conformity with the practices of the Western Church; but to Charlemagne's mind it went too far in encouraging the veneration of images, and he did not hesitate to say so.

Under Hadrian I and Charlemagne the relationship of pope to king still resembled alliance as much as dependence. Conflicts between them were rare: Charlemagne wrote to Hadrian, "Your interests are ours, and ours are yours." And Hadrian preserved the Church's moral independence by refusing to accept Charlemagne's criticisms of the Second Nicene Council. "We are more concerned," he wrote, "for the salvation of souls and the preservation of the true faith than for the possession of the world."

But Hadrian's successor, Leo III (795–816), was obliged to act otherwise. The papacy could raise its head morally only when the political situation in Italy was secure. But the security of Italy depended on the power of the Frankish king. Thus, the moral strength of the pope depended upon the king's being both strong and benevolent. This unhappy fact was demonstrated many times during the ninth century, but never more dramatically than in the events of 799–800.

At this time the popes were often members of one or another of

[3]Adoptionism is related to Nestorianism. The argument was that the Virgin gave birth to a wholly human Jesus, who was later "adopted" by God as his Son.

the great Roman noble families, who were frequently in deadly enmity. The enemies of Leo III's family ambushed the pope on April 25, 799, as he was riding through the city. They threw him off his horse, beat him savagely, and tried to blind him and cut off his tongue. Then, to justify their actions, they issued a public indictment accusing him of heresy and immorality. As his predecessors had called upon the Frankish king to help the Romans against the Lombards, so now Leo called upon Charlemagne for help against the Romans themselves.

The peace and tranquillity of Italy were too important to Charlemagne for him to ignore the summons, and he came down to Rome in the following year, 800. There he heard the accusations, sifted the evidence, and finally declared that he was convinced of Leo's innocence and that a public trial was unnecessary. By strong implication a Frankish king had sat in judgment upon a pope in the same way that the Byzantine emperor had used to do. On Christmas Day, 800, while Charlemagne was praying at Mass in the Cathedral of St. Peter, Leo rewarded him by placing upon the brow of the Teutonic ruler the imperial crown of Rome.

Historians have long debated the motives of the pope in granting, and of the king in accepting, the imperial honor. In point of fact, the significance of the coronation has varied according to the interpreter. For example, the pope's placing the crown upon the king's head might seem to imply that imperial powers were derived from the pope (at Christmas, 1804, Napoleon at his own imperial coronation seized the crown from the pope and placed it on his own head precisely in order to avoid this implication). Yet after Charlemagne was crowned, the pope fell down before him in the posture of submission with which his predecessors had signified their submission to the emperors of Rome. Theoretically the coronation could be interpreted as symbolizing either imperial or papal supremacy. In practice, it served primarily to enhance the prestige and power of the Frankish ruler.

So far had order prevailed over prophecy that the Church was now an integral part of the *imperium christianum,* defending its values and dependent upon its welfare. Christianity was a part of the kingdom of this world. In the course of the ninth century, the limitations of this situation were already evident. Following the death of Charlemagne in 814, the Frankish Empire fell asunder under the internal pressures of civil war and of dynastic division and dissension, combined with the external pressures of a new wave of raids and invasions mounted by Vikings, Moslems, and Magyars. By 900 no farm or town in Western Europe was safe from burning and ravaging by one or more of these peoples, and the stabilizing of European society that by 800 had seemed on the way was postponed for at least another century.

The natural consequence of dependence upon imperial power was that the Church shared the decline of the empire. A kind of pattern was produced, recurring at several stages in medieval history, in which the papacy, reformed and strengthened by a powerful and benevolent monarch and subject to that monarch's will, would continue to be strong for a while after the succession of a weaker ruler. There would be a short period of papal domination of the empire. Then, unable to support its own political independence, the papacy would also collapse and be obliged to await revival at the hands of a revived empire.

Thus, during the decline of the Frankish Empire, there was a succession of three powerful popes: Nicholas I (858–867), Hadrian II (867–872), and John VIII (872–882). These popes were able to press the reform of the Church, to force a bigamous emperor (Lothar II) to put away his second wife, and to issue statements of the theoretical supremacy of the spiritual over the temporal power. But the collapse of Carolingian power left the Roman nobles with a free hand, and in 882 the enemies of John VIII succeeded in bribing one of his servants to poison him. The poison proving not to be quick enough, the conspirators burst into the papal bedchamber and finished the job by beating out the pontiff's brains with a hammer. This outrage ushered in a long period of debasement. The papacy of the eighth century had been lifted up in the arms of the king of the Franks; the papacy of the tenth, still in the Frankish Empire's embrace, sank with it into the mire.

vi Christianity in Society, 700–1050

The religious justification of the integration of Christianity with society is that it makes it possible for religion to influence society more strongly. Does this justification withstand the test of practice? To what extent did the Christian ideals taught by the Church really affect the assumptions, attitudes, and actions of people in the medieval West? And, conversely, to what extent was Christianity transformed by the needs of society?

Incontrovertibly, most of the assumptions running through medieval literature and philosophy are Christian in origin. But writers in at least the early Middle Ages were almost all clergymen, and it is a question how far their attitudes represented those of the rest of the population. It is even difficult to penetrate to the deepest beliefs and opinions of the literate, because so much medieval writing was conventionally woven around the ideas, and even the language, of the Bible, the classics, and the Church fathers. Some medieval works are scarcely more than a string of allusions. However, we may assume that attitudes repeatedly expressed in a number of different ways by a variety of writers and artists have a general currency. Further, it is possible to penetrate beneath the explicit. Since people believe it unnecessary to express those things that seem most obvious and self-evident to them, it is the assumptions that are only implicit in their writing that are often the most fundamental.

Certain attitudes largely derived from Christianity not only had wide currency among the literate but commanded deep conviction even among the uneducated throughout the early Middle Ages. A sacred, rather than a profane, view of the world was generally assumed. Everything was created by God, and, as God was immanent in the world, everything was an expression of God. Yet the dualism inherent in Christianity, as well as simple observation of nature and of human nature, required that the world be mistrusted. Since the fall of Adam, not only man, but nature itself, was corrupt. Poets often used beautiful images derived from nature, but the images were expected to be understood metaphorically. For example, in a poem by Alcuin, a bird who has flown away from his home and lost his way is a symbol of a scholar who has gone out to study and not yet returned to his home monastery; or, on another level of meaning, the soul that has not yet found its way home to God. Nature as well as literature was interpreted on several levels, and it was not forgotten that this world was a temporary stage on our journey to the other.

The ideal of *peregrinatio* prevailed, therefore, with all its implications. The concerns of this world are vanity of vanities, and the proper attitude toward them is disengagement and contempt. Greatness was therefore measured differently in medieval society from the way it is measured in ours. It was not the man who changed the world who was great, but the one who in his proper place contributed to its order, or the one who learned how to rise above it. At first glance, there seems to the modern mind to be a paucity of great men in the Middle Ages, men whose characters and peculiarities are as well known to us as those of Alexander, Caesar, or Napoleon. This is not because such men did not exist, but because people found the deeds of obscure saints more worthy of admiration. Men who worked for order in the world by filling well their assigned place in society, like Gregory VII or Louis IX, received their due. But equally often it was the man of prophecy, the obscure ascetic or the mystic, who was considered great. There was no virtue in fame or worldly power. Artists, writers, architects, and sculptors often refrained from signing their work, which was offered in praise of God, not for the applause of the world. Medieval writers delighted in describing great kings or bishops whose wealth and power were suddenly brought to nothing by the hand of God; how, for example, on the death of William the Conqueror his supporters deserted him to seek out the new king, and his servants stripped the bed linen out from under the royal corpse. In the Middle Ages, holiness, rather than fame or wealth, was the way to obtain status. A more different attitude from that of the Renaissance or of the twentieth century is difficult to imagine.

Yet gradually the idea that the whole world was sacred was transformed. The institutionalization of Christianity encouraged the Church gradually to recognize the existence of the profane (the marketplace) and to distinguish between it and the sacred (the church or the monastery). Even nature became secularized. The ancients considered man a part of nature; Augustine had affirmed God's immanence in all things natural. But Christianity also taught that God had made the world for man. This notion, together with the rapid growth of technology in the early Middle Ages, brought about exploitation of nature, in place of reverence for it. Today, we find wholly natural man's manipulation of the world, which has almost eliminated wilderness, tamed natural forces, and destroyed ecological balance. But this attitude seems to have emerged in the course of the eighth and ninth centuries. It is exemplified in the change in the pictures on calendars: earlier, the months were represented by the appropriate natural phenomena—winds in March, falling leaves in November, or snow in January. Later, the pictures represented the human actions appropriate to that month—tilling, sowing, or harvesting. This attitude both sprang from and encouraged the great development of technology in the medieval, and then in the modern, world.

Thus the spirit of order as well as that of prophecy came to be at work as men recognized the reality of the world and the necessity of living in it. Human society was considered static, and political and legal systems were supposed to reflect the unchanging divine order of things. There was an absolute divine moral law, which the human mind could find both in revelation and in the rational principles of right reason (natural law). Men believed that they did not *make* law; they *discovered* it. Their task was to construct human legislation and administration in accordance with divine law. When human laws conformed to divine law, they were considered "just"; when they did not, they were considered "unjust" and consequently null and void. In practice, of course, laws were introduced and changed to meet new conditions. But these changes were never thought of as progressive, but rather as a return to pristine purity. For example, Henry II of England, who made sweeping innovations in the administrative and legal systems of his country, always maintained (and possibly believed) that he was simply returning to the good old laws of his grandfather Henry I.

Medieval respect for order was reinforced by excessive reverence for the past. There was little sense of progress. The culmination of the world would be the Second Coming and Last Judgment, but these would be cosmic, not historical, events. Augustine had elaborated a theory of time and of history that provided for the idea of progress, but this proved uncongenial to all but a very few sophisticated historians like St. Bede. For the most part, medieval men ignored the idea that human events were leading anywhere and preferred the venerable and almost universally held tradition of the ancients that the Golden Age lay in the past. For the medieval mind there were two manifestations of the Golden Age: the primitive, apostolic Church, golden in its purity; and classical

Rome, golden in its splendor and intellectual achievements. The writings of the fathers of the Church on the one hand, and of the classical philosophers and poets on the other, were credited with enormous authority. As Bernard of Chartres respectfully remarked, "We are but ants on the shoulders of giants." Disputes in theology were referred to the Church fathers, and disputes in medicine to Galen. Men who wanted their writing taken seriously indulged in a kind of reverse plagiarism and passed it off as a newly discovered work of one of the ancients.

The Greek conception of an orderly cosmos prevailed in the Middle Ages. It was a universe immeasurably simpler than ours: a stationary earth round which revolved the concentric spheres of moon, sun, planets, and stars. Everything in the universe, according to the Aristotelian doctrine followed in the Middle Ages, had its proper and appointed place. On earth, everything seeks its own place by moving, unless inhibited, in a straight line. Fire is the lightest element and strives always to rise; if one picks up a stone, holds it aloft, and then drops it, it will seek to return to its proper place as quickly as it can.

Human society was as static and orderly as the cosmos, and numerous writers (for example, Pseudo-Dionysius the Areopagite, a sixth-century monk) wrote treatises comparing the earthly hierarchy with the heavenly. In fact there were three social hierarchies, the feudal-manorial, the urban, and the ecclesiastical. Within this ordered society, every institution and every person had *libertas*. The meaning of *libertas* was quite different from the meaning of "liberty" now. It meant the right—and the duty—of an individual to occupy his proper place in society. A carpenter ought not to try to become a knight; on the other hand, no one ought to deprive him of his proper status as carpenter. In practice, of course, people did change professions and gained or lost status; but theory, reinforced by the practical demands of the feudal-manorial system, did much to inhibit social mobility. Curiously, it was within the Church, the institution most devoted to hierarchy and order, that a man might most easily improve his lot. Bishops often gave scholarships to poor boys of intelligence, and only within the Church could a son of a serf or a penniless freeman rise to prominence and power. Even when most conservative, the Church remembered Christ's admonition that it was what was within a man, rather than his outward appearance, that was important.

The assumptions of Christianity appear everywhere in medieval thought and culture, but they had competition.

The practical demands of the agricultural economy and of military organization had created a feudal system, whose code of ethics, chivalry, evolved not often contradictory to Christianity but different in its emphasis. For example, the fundamental vice in Christian thought is pride, but, since feudalism depended upon loyalty to one's lord, treachery was the worst thing imaginable to the feudal mind. Gradually these ideas colored Christian values. Christ was frequently depicted as a feudal seigneur. Our duty is to remain personally loyal to him as if in fulfillment of a feudal contract; if we break that contract, we take the consequences bravely and go to hell. In much Christian thought it is Satan's treachery to his lord, God, that is particularly evil, and in the *Divine Comedy* it is traitors who share with him the lowest depths of hell: Brutus, Cassius, and Judas Iscariot.

Among the peasants, Christianity was limited by many traditional values derived from paganism and from ancient agricultural traditions. In the later Middle Ages, the expansion of commerce, rise of the towns, and consequent emergence of a class of merchants and industrialists promoted the rise of an ethic based upon worldly material success and respectability; and one of the more curious episodes in the history of morality is the coloration by this worldly, bourgeois ethic of a Christianity whose spirit was originally otherworldly and revolutionary.

The establishment of an officially Christian society promoted and enforced the spread of Christian values within society; but at the same time it encouraged the adjustment of these values to those arising from other sources of society.

The *Song of Roland,* written in French near the end of the eleventh century, illustrates the mingling of non-Christian with Christian attitudes in a poem that is at first sight wholly Christian. The story is well known: Charlemagne wishes to convert the Moslems of Spain to Christianity by peaceful means. But he sends to the court of the Moslem king, Marsila, a treacherous ambassador named Ganelon. Ganelon deliberately misrepresents Charlemagne's proposals to Marsila, saying that the Franks' real purpose is to turn half of Spain into a fief for Count Roland. Ganelon is motivated by his violent hatred for Roland, Charlemagne's favorite adviser and comrade-in-arms. Roland is Ganelon's stepson, and they have had long and bitter disputes over family and property. Encouraged by Ganelon, who agrees to see to it that part of the Christian host is betrayed to them, the Moslems defy Charlemagne, who invades Spain. The war is inconclusive, and the Frankish army begins to return northward across the Pyrenees. By Ganelon's contrivance, Charlemagne leaves a rear guard at the Pass of Roncesvalles under the command of Count Roland to cover his retreat; this rear guard is set upon by a vast army of Moslems who, completely outnumbering them, defeat and kill them all. Charlemagne appears at the scene of the battle too late to save Roland but in time to destroy the Moslem army and avenge the death of his comrade.

On the surface, the poem looks like a call to crusade. The Moslems are described as idolaters and devil-worshipers; they practice black magic; and some of them are black, twisted, and demonic in appearance. The war is a war for Christianity against Islam, of good against evil, of light against darkness. Yet in that war the Christian hero was slain; and even after his final victory, Charlemagne complained, " 'How toilsome is my life!' / And wept, and tore in sorrow his white beard."[1]

[1]Frederick Bliss Luquiens, trans., *The Song of Roland* (New York, 1952), p. 101.

Christian values have really little place in the poem. The only man of the cloth among the characters is Archbishop Turpin, who is too zestfully occupied with warfare to concern himself with mercy and charity. "A curse on him who smites not rudely now!"[2] he calls out in battle; and he has little time for blessings, even for those who lie dying. The characters perfunctorily observe the Christian externals: Charlemagne goes to Mass, and Roland confesses before he dies. But by no stretch of the imagination is this a deeply Christian poem. The dead Roland is borne directly up to heaven by the archangels Michael and Gabriel, in the manner not of a penitent Christian, but of a pagan hero borne off by the Valkyries to Valhalla.

For a poem calling for a Christian crusade against Islam, the Moslems are often strangely admirable. They appear less often as black idolaters than as noble warriors worthy of their opponents' steel. Here the influence of classical humanism is evident: the author of the poem has in mind the *Iliad* or at least the second book of the *Aeneid*. The battle scenes, in which personal struggles between one brave warrior and another are featured seriatim, and the name Priam improbably borne by one of the Moslem nobles, indicate that the author was thinking of the war between the Greeks and the Trojans. He draws many parallels between the two sides: the Moslem king, Marsila, is a just, honorable, and dignified ruler, like Charlemagne, and like Charlemagne he surrounds himself with a council of advisers. The Moslems fight for "fair Spain," the Franks for "France the sweet." The war is brought on by the evil counsel and treachery of false advisers: Ganelon on the French side and Blanchandrin on the Spanish. The poem is charged, like a Greek tragedy, with the sense of brooding and ineluctable fate. Charlemagne has a dream warning him of the evil consequences of the expedition, nor does he trust the traitor Ganelon; yet he is powerless to stop the fatal train of events. Roland, affected by the classical tragic flaw of overweening pride, refuses to blow his horn

[2]*Ibid.*, p. 72.

for rescue until it is too late, and Nemesis pursues him to his inevitable death.

The poem is also deeply chivalric. The great virtues are to fight well and to die well. Cowardice brings dishonor, and to yield in battle is worse than death. The great sin is treachery, and for that sin Ganelon dies a hideous death. Charles first orders that he be hanged like Judas on an accursed tree; but the judges demand that he be tied to four horses who, when they are driven apart, pull his body asunder. Even Ganelon's defense before the king's court is feudal: he argues that because he openly threw down the gauntlet of defiance, he was entitled to pursue his feud with Roland to the death.

Even as feudal values permeate the supposedly Christian epic of Roland, they also permeated the entire structure of the Church, from the papacy down to the smallest parish. The rulers protected and patronized the Church because of their desire for order in society and their need of well-trained administrators; they were not as a whole indifferent to spiritual values, but they insisted that these take second place to the practical needs of society. As long as the Church insisted upon retaining wealth and temporal power, so long would the kings need to use it as a tool of social control.

The welfare of the papacy during the tenth and early eleventh century depended upon the protection of the emperor. But the emperors continued to be almost powerless until 962, when Otto the Great of Germany conquered Italy. A successor later added Burgundy, and for centuries the kings of Germany simultaneously possessed the titles of king of Italy and king of Burgundy. In 963, Otto assumed the imperial title as well. As Charlemagne had sat in judgment upon Pope Leo III, Otto the Great sat in judgment upon Pope John XII, accused by his enemies of heresy and paganism as well as of immorality. Otto at first declared John innocent but, after John had broken several political promises to the emperor, finally deposed him. This was the first deposition of a pope by an emperor since Martin I had been removed by the Byzantine emperor in the seventh century.

But the kings of Germany were much occupied north of the Alps; and with the Italian political situation being so extremely complex, particularly in the cities of Lombardy, they could not often guarantee the stability of Rome. As a result, the papacy was commonly at the disposal of the Roman nobility, which selected popes on political and venal grounds. Many of the popes of the tenth century were monsters of depravity that exceeded the brutality of the least admirable popes of the Renaissance. Of one pontiff it was said that he turned the papal palace into a brothel and that pilgrims ceased visiting the shrine of St. Peter lest they be ravished by his successor.

The bishops were integrated into the feudal political system in a variety of ways, all of which interfered in their spiritual functions. In the first place, they continued to serve as administrators for the state. Kings relied upon bishops and archbishops for advice at meetings of the royal council; and they employed bishops as chancellors or other officials in the central government. Further, much local authority was entrusted to the bishops. The Carolingians had established as local governors the counts (with jurisdiction over civil affairs), the dukes (with largely military jurisdiction), and the bishops (sometimes with both). In France, for example, Reims, Laon, Langres, and Noyon were completely under the control and jurisdiction of bishops; and in other cities throughout Europe the bishops either had complete power or shared power with lay lords. This civil responsibility of the bishops was a direct continuation of that which they had acquired during the decline of the old Roman Empire. A society in which political authority was weak and decentralized needed the support of whatever institutions commanded any kind of respect or obedience. The kings came to rely upon the bishops more than upon any other single institution for the maintenance of public order; and for precisely this reason, they had to make sure that only bishops whom they could trust were elected.

There were other reasons why the kings needed to control the bishops. In the same way that the popes were building the patrimony of St. Peter, each bishop was building up the personal possessions of his own see. Technically such possessions did not belong to the individual bishop or even to the bishopric, but to the patron saint of the diocese. At Liège in Belgium, for example, episcopal possessions were known as the patrimony of St. Lambert, and, there as elsewhere, the good saint laid up many treasures on earth.

There were several sources of these possessions: (1) Many wealthy people tried to buy their way out of sin by giving gifts of money or land to a church, either during their lifetime or as a bequest. These gifts were sometimes given in the form of "divine service," by which the saint was to hold the land as long as certain spiritual services were rendered the donor (for example, he might ask that Mass be said for him weekly or daily); or the gifts might take the form of "free alms"—land given, again for pious purposes, with no duties whatever attached. (2) The bishop had sources of revenue that often rendered him wealthy, and he might use these moneys to add to the patrimony by purchase. (3) More rarely, land could be occupied by brute force, or confiscated as a result of a legal judgment in court.

The patrimony was held free and clear by the Church and owed no military or monetary service to the king. So much land passed to the Church that at some periods as much as a quarter of Western Europe was in its hands. The kings were therefore obliged to confiscate Church property, as did Charles Martel; to order that no more land be given the Church, as did Edward I (1272–1307) in his Statute of Mortmain;[3] or at least to make doubly sure that bishops were men they could trust.

But the patrimony was by no means all of the land held by a bishop, and often it was not the most important part. The bishop frequently held territories in feudal tenure. That is to say, he was granted lands, just like a lay lord, in return for the execution of feudal duties, including military service. A bishop holding such

[3]*Mortmain,* the term for such Church property, literally means "dead hand," referring to the fact that it gave the king no advantage.

land was obliged, every bit as much as a count or a baron, to come when called to the royal army and to provide the king with the number of warriors requisite to the amount of land he held. Usually the bishops sent their troops without going into battle themselves, but Archbishop Turpin in the *Song of Roland* is not a fantastic figure. St. Boniface had to reprimand a bishop for slicing off the head of a family enemy; Bishop Odo of Bayeux was a bloody and unscrupulous fighter; and the bishops of Liège not infrequently appeared in the imperial host.

As administrators, as the possessors of enormous Church properties, and as feudal lords, therefore, the bishops had so much wealth and power that the kings could not afford not to control them. The German kings depended upon the support of the bishops more than upon any other single group, except perhaps the towns. The French kings gradually, through the eleventh and twelfth century, added to the number of sees to which they might directly appoint. The system was self-perpetuating: the more power and wealth the bishops had, the more the kings needed to appoint loyal men; but to secure and preserve the loyalty of such men, the kings had to bestow upon them further power and wealth. It is no wonder that the bishops kept their eyes more attentively upon the throne than upon the cross.

The diocese of Liège is a good example of the enormous temporal complications of a powerful bishopric. Liège was a village until the eighth century, when, owing to certain disputes, the bishop of Tongres moved his see there. The bishop gathered clergy round him, tradesmen and artisans came to serve the clergy, and the population grew. The location proved to be a good one, near the land route between the Rhine and Flanders, and by the early tenth century the city was of some economic and political consequence.

Liège is located in Wallonie, the French-speaking part of modern Belgium, but in the Middle Ages Wallonie was part of the kingdom of Germany. Ecclesiastically, Liège was part of the province of Cologne, whose archbishop was the immediate ecclesiastical superior of the bishop of Liège. Politically, Liège lay in that part of Germany known as Lower Lorraine. But the duke of Lorraine was never very powerful, and his duchy was divided into numerous little counties and baronies, all relatively independent. Lorraine was a rich province, and the king of Germany wanted to control it securely, yet he was puzzled as to the means of doing so. The dukes were weak and often hostile, and the lesser nobility too disunited. If he were to control the area at all, the king had to rely upon the bishops.

In Lower Lorraine the two most important sees for political purposes were those of Cologne and Liège. Otto the Great appointed his younger brother Bruno as archbishop of Cologne (953–965), and Bruno proved a loyal and effective viceroy, extending his influence even into France. But the kings did not have enough brothers to staff every diocese in the kingdom, and they were obliged to secure other support. In 972–1008, the diocese of Liège was under the rule of a brilliant bishop, Notger. Notger undertook public works to improve the city, erected fortifications, cleared the countryside of robbers, improved the order and discipline of his churches, and founded an episcopal school that began to attract scholars from all over Europe. By the end of the century, Liège was one of the great intellectual and artistic centers of northern Europe.

Notger and his successors also took pains to increase the patrimony of St. Lambert and to improve their political situation. They entered readily into an alliance with the emperor. The deal was simple: The bishop of Liège would act as the king's supporter and administrator; in return, the king would protect and support the bishop of Liège and give him grants of land and money. The king wanted the petty nobility of the province brought into order; the bishop wanted to annex their territories. The policy recommending itself was simple: the king would support the bishop's conquest of his neighbors.

By conquest and by purchase, then, the power of the bishops was extended up and down the Meuse River and its tributaries. The count of Liège gradually lost his powers and was eliminated; the county of Huy was annexed; and dozens of smaller fiefs shared the same fate. Nor were the purchases of property more edifying: when Bishop Otbert (1091–1119) bought the castle of Bouillon from Count Godfrey, he raised the money from his parish priests, who had to sell their churches' ornaments and squeeze the rest out of their parishioners. In the meanwhile, Liège became the firmest ally of the kings. It was at Liège that the Emperor Henry IV, pursued by a victorious and vengeful alliance consisting of his own son, the barons, and the pope, found final refuge; it was there, in the last loyal city in his kingdom, that he died in 1106. Liège retained its political independence till the French Revolution; and a great monument on the Meuse still honors the wars not of Belgium, but of Liège—from 1105, when the Liégeois repulsed the old emperor's enemies at the Battle of Visé, to the war of 1939–1945.

The worldly preoccupations of the bishop of Liège may be imagined. He was the spiritual director of the diocese of Liège and, as such, the head of a complicated diocesan administration. The diocese was divided into archdeaconries, each archdeacon having spiritual jurisdiction over the parishes in his archdeaconry. At the city of Liège itself sat the bishop at his cathedral. There also was the "great archdeacon," who controlled the financial matters of the diocese, and the cathedral chapter, which consisted of the priests living at the cathedral and occupying themselves with the administration of the diocese. The chapter was headed by a dean, and both dean and archdeacon often proved rivals to the bishop for authority. Throughout the diocese stretched a complicated system of ecclesiastical law courts and church schools.

But in addition to being spiritual head of a diocese, the bishop was also prince of his temporal possessions, including the patrimony and his feudal holdings. These were scattered throughout the diocese, making up about a fourth to a third of its territory, the rest being still in the hands of the lay nobility. As prince, the bishop was the head of a complicated civil administration, with its own officers and law courts. This administration was parallel to, but independent of, the ecclesiastical structure. As prince, the bishop was responsible not only for internal administration but for the fulfillment of his feudal duties to his overlord, the king of Germany. The bishop was obliged, exactly like any lay lord, to send troops to the king for his campaigns. When Bishop Wazo failed to send military aid to King Henry III during a campaign against the rebellious count of Holland, the king summoned him to court and reprimanded him publicly. Wazo's plea that his spiritual duties had prevented him from participating in the campaign did not visibly impress the king, and his suggestion that a bishop's spiritual functions were more important than his temporal was greeted with disbelief and, one may suppose, astonishment.

Under these circumstances, the interference of temporal with spiritual concerns was massive. Nor was such interference limited to the bishops. The monasteries, which also possessed wealth and wide lands, were also a tempting plum for the kings, many of whom simply caused themselves to be elected abbots. King Hugh Capet of France (987–996), for example, was abbot of the rich monastery of Saint-Denis, north of Paris.

The ideal of a Christian society was transformed, and not subtly, by worldly concerns. The desire of the spirit of order was not to withdraw from or to spurn the world, but to convert it. Now in order to convert society, a Church must to some extent meet society on society's terms. The balance between aloofness from the world to the point of seeing it as irrelevant and mixing with the world to the point of compromise is always difficult to maintain, and inevitably a certain coarseness crept into a Church that had to deal with a coarse society.

There were monasteries that drifted away from observance of the rule, allowing the monks to wander about at will. Among the bishops the most common sin was simony, the buying and selling of ecclesiastical offices. All too often a king would give a diocese to a man who promised a lump sum, a share of the revenues, or at least loyal political support; and the new bishop would recoup his losses by selling attractive parishes to the highest bidders or by otherwise extracting money from the faithful. Things were no better in the villages, where lay feudal lords often obtained possession of parish churches—churches of their manors, churches they had built, or churches given them by another feudal lord or by the king. These laymen were known as "lay proprietors," and they had much the same kind of control over the parish priests that the king had over the bishops. They selected the priests themselves and either sold them the parishes or else hired them at a small percentage of the parish revenues. Like the simoniac bishops, these priests had to recover their outlay, and in violation of the canon law, they frequently sold the sacraments (another variety of simony), refusing to bury or baptize without pay. Such priests were often illiterate, lived openly with women, frequented taverns, and otherwise lived lives that not only did not inspire but sometimes revolted their parishioners.

It is of course easy to exaggerate the corruption of the Church. The priests and monks who were living orderly and decent lives did not attract attention. It is equally clear, however, that the corruption we have described was neither isolated nor atypical. The effect upon the morale and the morality of the Christian people may be imagined. It is scarcely surprising that disaffection from the Church was not uncommon.

The decline of the liturgy was a most important element in this disaffection. The liturgy was the public worship of the Christian people, and from the time of the earliest Church it was centered upon the Mass. The Mass was the gathering of the people of Christ in brotherhood around the table of the Lord, where the sacrifice of Calvary was reproduced and where the bread and wine, having been transformed into the body and blood of Christ, were received by the people in Holy Communion. The Mass was the occasion of the offering up of the self to God in the form of the unconsecrated bread and wine and the receiving back of the consecrated bread and wine now become Christ. It was a sacrament that was simple, understandable to the people, and reverent. It was a service of the community gathered together, uniting them in love and fellowship.

In the earliest Church, the Mass was in Greek; but as early as the fourth century, the language was changed to Latin throughout western Europe, in order that the people might understand it. But by the end of the seventh century, ordinary uneducated people no longer understood Latin; and the ignorance of many priests was such that they were unable not only to understand but even to recite the words properly. As a result, the Mass was presented to the people not as the life-giving word of God, but as an unintelligible mumbling. Further, the growing wealth and prestige of the clergy persuaded them to emphasize the separation between them and the people, and churches consequently became larger and more formal. The table of the Lord was removed from the center of the congregation and placed at one end of the church, where the priest said Mass with his back to the people. In large churches, a choir and even a choir screen separated the congregation from the altar, rendering the service sometimes invisible as well as unintelligible. An altar rail emphasized the separation of the people from the Lord's table. The congregation ceased to make the responses to the priest, this function being taken over by altar boys, who, like the priests, usually mumbled incomprehensibly. The processions ceased in which the people had come forward to offer their gifts, and free gifts were replaced by compulsory tithes. Attendance at Mass was probably quite low, and Communion, originally weekly for everyone, became so infrequent that councils were obliged to set forth the rule that one must go to Communion at least once a year under pain of sin. As the Mass lost much of its meaning to most ordinary Christians, the religious life of the Church was diverted more and more into private devotions, peripheral cults, and externals. Genuflections, the rosary, private prayers, or the veneration of saints filled the needs of a people deprived of more substantial spiritual fare.

But an age or an institution is not to be judged by its failures, or everything would be worthy of condemnation. Judgment is better made in terms of the vigor of the institution in taking measures to combat and to overcome those failures. Even in the darkest moments of the Church, when the attempt to achieve order had degenerated into disorder, the spirits both of true order and of prophecy demanded reform. Against the superstition and the corruption, the voice of a purer Christian spirit was never silent.

vii Reform

One of the most impressive features of the Church is its perennial ability to reform itself. At no time, even when the morality and the morale of the Church were at their lowest, did movements of reform cease to animate and quicken its spirit. These movements were necessary because on the one hand no alternative to Christianity was thinkable, and on the other it was unthinkable to tolerate for long a distorted Christianity. The Christian view of time and history facilitated reform movements. Men looked back to the age of the apostles and the Church fathers as a Golden Age of purity, and accordingly they tried to reform—"re-form" in the sense of recreating this past. But the Christian belief in development and direction in history now added another dimension to reform: it was not merely a return to the past but a *reformatio in melius,* a bit of progress—still on the model of the past, but a small step ahead.

There have always been movements of reform in the Church, but from the time of St. Boniface they grew in numbers and in strength. The impetus to morality, education, and discipline given the Christian community by the missionaries and their royal Frankish collaborators stimulated a vigorous response to corruption and decay. There was too little continuity among these responses to speak of them as one great movement, but they were all parts of a general thrust to reestablish true Christianity against intolerable conditions.

There were two kinds of reform, usually cooperating with each other and often unaware of the differences between them in their attack upon the common enemy, yet quite distinct. One was reform based upon the precepts of order. The reformers of this variety argued that the trouble was found in the disorder of the Church and that disorder could be cured by means of discipline. This discipline was to be achieved by strengthening the authority of the Church and bolstering the power and efficiency of those in charge of the Christian society. Reformers of order might support the pope or the bishops as the most proper authorities to lead Christian society; or they might equally well support the emperor or the kings; but they were all agreed that what was needed was the obedience of the Christian people to just and proper authority. The arguments of order dominated political as well as theological theory. One historian of medieval political thought, Walter Ullmann, calls their point of view the "descending theory" of authority: God delegates his authority to an earthly vicar (the emperor or the pope, depending upon one's point of view), who in turn delegates it to his officers, secular authority to temporal lords and spiritual authority to ecclesiastical lords. In order to be in conformity with God's will, one has only to obey his superiors. If by chance they should err, they bear the responsibility for their error, but their inferiors are not to reason why.

The other kind of reform sprang from the prophetic spirit. To the prophet, order was of subsidiary importance or even a positive evil. The law of God is written in the hearts of men, and the need for an earthly authority is minimal. As the Kingdom of God is not of this world, our chief concern should be not to improve the world, but to rise above it. The prophetic spirit was fond of citing from the Gospels the story of Mary and Martha. When Jesus visited the sisters, Martha busied herself about the house, cleaning up and cooking dinner, while Mary sat at Jesus' feet listening. At last Martha grew annoyed and asked her sister to help, but Jesus replied, "Martha, Martha, thou art troubled and busy with many things, but one thing is needful: and Mary has chosen that good part." In other words, though good works in the world are desirable, the higher vocation is meditation upon the world of God. The prophetic spirit looked with indifference upon the struggles of pope and emperor for the control of Christian society and was unimpressed by the papalists' argument that the root of evil was lay influence in the ecclesiastical order. The ecclesiastical order itself was superfluous; the Holy Spirit within was to guide men's lives. The prophetic variety of reform was always the voice of a small minority which flourished among monks, mystics, and heretics; yet, oddly, many of the prophets commanded great respect in a society that, however much concerned with the things of this world, never wholly forgot the other.

There were three major sources of reform in the years between Boniface's mission and the papal revolution that began about 1050: the kings, the monasteries, and the laity.

Royal leadership of reform was of course concerned with the creation of order, and within the context of order, it was perfectly natural. There was the long tradition of imperial control of the Church that stretched back to Constantine. There was the practical consideration that only kings had the wealth and the power to enforce reform. And ordinarily the kings had proper intentions. Most of them were sincere Christians; and they recognized the value of the Church for education and administration. There were plenty of opportunities for exploitation of the Church: for example, simony, the confiscation of Church properties, or the diversion of Church revenues. But most rulers wished to build and maintain an upright Church, so long as their own control of it was retained. When the papalists later argued that corruption was the result of lay interference in the Church, they forgot that lay interference had also produced most of the reform.

Among the Franks, the reform traditions of Boniface were continued by Pepin the Short, his son Charlemagne, and his grandson Louis the Pious (814–840). Convinced by advisers like Alcuin that the Frankish state could revive the vigor and glory of the Roman Empire, Charlemagne set about to make his capital, Aachen, an intellectual center and the Frankish Church a model of efficiency and purity. The zeal that led Charlemagne to attack the Avars, Saxons, and Spanish Moors was religious as well as political and military in motivation, and he and his advisers were as determined to continue the internal improvement of the Church as to extend the geographical boundaries of Christendom.

Charlemagne and his son Louis the Pious strove to restore discipline to the monasteries by reestablishing the rule of St. Benedict. They supported the efforts of another Benedict, St. Benedict of Aniane, to force lapsed Benedictine monasteries back to strict obedience to the rule and to bring under the rule houses that had not yet accepted it. By decree of the council of Aachen in 816, only the Benedictine rule was to be recognized in the kingdom of the Franks. This was a triumph of regularity not only in the Frankish kingdom but, owing to the vast prestige of the Franks, throughout western Europe.

In their great council the Frankish kings issued capitularies concerning every aspect of society including the Church, and these capitularies seconded and wrote into civil law the injunctions of Church councils against immorality.

When after 870 the kingdom was divided, generally speaking, into a kingdom of the West Franks (later France) and a kingdom of the East Franks (later Germany), the rulers of those countries continued to support reform as long as they were powerful enough to do so. In Germany, Otto the Great and his successors held a series of national councils in which the Church supported royal policy in return for strong royal efforts for reform. Otto III (983–1002) had as tutors some of the great reforming monks, and the young king demonstrated what he had learned by appointing one of the few worthy popes of the period, Gerbert of Aurillac (Sylvester II, 999–1003), a monk, scholar, and reformer. The efforts of Henry II (1002–1024) and Henry III (1039–1056) on behalf of order were so great that both of them were canonized.

The kings continued to support educational as well as moral advance. The West Frankish court of Charles the Bald (843–877) was almost as brilliant as that of Charlemagne itself; and in Germany the Ottos encouraged intellectual activity at court, in the episcopal schools like that of Liège, and in monasteries like Fulda, founded by Boniface, which became in the tenth century one of the intellectual centers of Germany.

The kings of England were even more attached to reform than their Frankish counterparts. Alfred the Great (871–899) developed his own intellectual court; one of the few early medieval monarchs who could read, he himself translated from Latin into English the *Dialogues* of Gregory the Great, the *Consolation of Philosophy* by Boethius, and other works. His successors, notably Edgar the Peaceful (959–975), strongly supported the monastic reforms of St. Dunstan and made efforts to appoint competent and moral bishops.

But royal reform, no matter how sincere, was postulated upon the demands of public order. The reforms centered in the monasteries were at once more prophetic, more vigorous, and often less enduring. Monastic reform at first was part of the royal program, witness the support of Charlemagne and Louis the Pious for the Benedictine order. But in the latter part of the ninth century, royal power was shattered and as incapable of promoting reform as it was of doing anything else. Accordingly, independent and spontaneous movements sprang up in the monasteries themselves.

Reforming monasteries arose all over Europe, but there were

three chief centers of activity: the Low Countries and the Rhineland; Burgundy; and northern Italy. Why these areas should have been the centers of reform is not certain, but there is probably a correlation with the fact that they were important economic and intellectual centers as well.

Monastic reform was itself based in part upon order and in part upon prophecy. The reformers wished to restore the *libertas* of the monasteries, that is, their proper place in the Christian *ordo*. To this end they sought to eliminate lay abbots and to remove the influence of lay proprietors and even of bishops. Accordingly they aligned themselves with the papacy, placing themselves directly under the authority of distant Rome in order to escape closer and more effective authorities. The result was, for better or for worse, to make the great abbots almost independent. But the more important goal of monastic reform was the restoration of the spiritual life. It was for this purpose that St. Gerard of Brogne (d. 959), for example, withdrew from the world and founded an ascetic monastery on his wealthy father's estate in the diocese of Cambrai. It was for this reason that at Camaldoli and at Fonte Avellana in Italy, monks withdrew into eremitical isolation. To St. Guthlac, alone and filthy on his island in the East Anglian fens, or to St. Romuald who emerged from the marshes of Italy with a green color induced by swamp gases, only direct communication between the individual and his God seemed to fulfill the injunctions of the Gospel to leave all one has and follow Christ.

But the curse of the Church is that nothing fails like success. Those monasteries that achieved the greatest influence and spread reform most broadly were themselves most subject to decline. The two most successful centers of monastic reform were Cluny in Burgundy and Gorze in Lorraine, each of which became the model and center of a large organization of daughter houses. Gorze, founded about 933 by St. John of Gorze with the help of Bishop Adalbero of Metz, exercised its influence upon over a hundred houses in Germany, Austria, and northern Italy. Cluny was as spectacular in the south, and it serves as a good example of both the success and the difficulties of monastic reform.

With the help of Duke William the Pious of Aquitaine, St. Berno, the wealthy son of a noble, withdrew from the world and in 909 founded the abbey of Cluny in Burgundy, restoring there the strict observance of the Rule of St. Benedict. The reaction of the feudal nobility to this foundation indicates that among even the wealthy laity who had most profited from the corruption of the Church, respect for the spirit was strong. Large donations of money and land flowed in, knights and great nobles came to make retreats at Cluny and to seek spiritual advice from its monks; and monks themselves were attracted in great numbers to the pure life. Under Abbot Odo (926–942), Berno's successor, the pope granted Cluny immunity from the authority of the bishops and placed it directly under the protection of Rome. Odo continued to cultivate the support of the wealthy and influential, and many lay proprietors of monasteries turned their powers over to him. By the time of Odo's death seventeen houses, including the influential monastery of Fleury, were under the authority of Cluny.

Under Abbot Maieul (954–994) and Abbot Odilo (994–1048), the number of such houses rose past a hundred, and a complex organization had to be set up for their administration. The abbot of Cluny retained authority over all the houses, each one of which had a prior in charge who was responsible to the abbot and subject to visitation by the abbot or his representatives. In the meantime gifts from the wealthy flowed in and an enormous and elaborate abbey was erected; and the abbot of Cluny, now next to popes and kings the most influential man in Europe, there received in splendor the great and the powerful from all over Europe. By imperceptible stages, Cluny began to drift away from the strict observance of the rule and to prefer power and wealth to humility and poverty. In the twelfth century, it was itself the target for a new generation of reformers. St. Bernard, remarking with disgust the splendors of their sumptuous church, warned the Cluniacs that they bedecked their walls with gold and jewels at the expense of the spiritual needs of the poor.

By the mid-eleventh century, in fact, monasticism was entering a most serious crisis, against which the policies of even an uncorrupted Cluny would be insufficient. Since the sixth century, the monasteries had been one of the most important pillars of Christian order. They were centers of calm and tranquillity. They were agriculturally productive. They were far and away the most important centers of education, producing scholars, artists, and administrators, as well as monks, for all of Europe. But by 1050 society was undergoing profound changes. The long economic depression that had begun in the third century had come to an end, and a new age of rapidly expanding population, growing towns, and flourishing industry and commerce began. The eleventh through the thirteenth centuries are a period of population and economic growth absolutely unparalleled in the history of the West until the nineteenth and twentieth centuries. Rapid population growth provoked rapid social changes. Political order was more secure than it had been since the age of the Antonines in the second century, and governments were rapidly expanding their powers and services.

The rise of the towns and of the merchant and artisan classes created new educational requirements: the sons and daughters of merchants needed to be trained at least to keep accounts. Growing wealth provided leisure and the inclination to pursue other things than food and war; and among these distractions, as well as games, hunting, and lecherous dalliance, were philosophy and the arts. The episcopal schools, located in the flourishing towns, now outstripped the bucolic monasteries in numbers, size, and importance. To the great cities flocked scholars from different lands; and with the exchange of ideas, new questions were formulated and new intellectual attitudes developed. Even the other social services of the monasteries—aid to the poor, the lodging of travelers, the care of widows and orphans, and the treatment of disease—were taken over by others. A growing economy provided more jobs and reduced the proportion of the needy and consequently the need for almsgiving. Widows, orphans, and the disabled were often provided for by guilds or by other voluntary religious organizations. With the growth of commerce, inns sprang up along the roads and rivers, providing lodging often jollier than that offered by the monasteries.

Medicine was now taught in the schools, and professional physicians, however incompetent by our standards, proved preferable to the care most monasteries could offer.

The effect of these social changes was greatly to reduce the social utility of the monasteries. The result was a crisis in monasticism and a subsequent reorientation of the monastic life. From the ninth to the end of the eleventh century, the only rule permitted in the West had been that of St. Benedict; now it was replaced by a number of others. More importantly, the fading of the monastic contribution to order opened the way for a revival in the monasteries of the spirit of prophecy. The less devoted found more congenial occupations in the growing cities or elsewhere; those who remained were no longer charged with so many social responsibilities; and the monasteries turned back to asceticism, meditation, and mysticism.

From the eighth to the eleventh centuries, however, the spirit of prophecy, often uncongenial to a Church seeking order, was frequently driven into dissent. There were no great movements of religious dissent until the twelfth century, but the earlier period produced numerous deviations of individuals or of small groups. A strict theological definition of heresy is a "doctrine tenaciously held against the doctrine of the Church," but dissent went far beyond theological heresy. The practice of strange rites and superstitious cults was equally a sign of disaffection. The chief distinction between medieval and ancient dissent is that whereas the heresies of the early Church were chiefly concerned with points, sometimes fine points, of theology, those of the medieval Church were chiefly concerned with moral questions. The heresies of the early Church were debated by priests and bishops in schools and synods; those of the Middle Ages were often propounded by laymen in the fields and marketplaces.

The nature of dissent reflected the state of society. The chief concerns of the Church in the years 700–1050 were corruption and reform. The dissenters were themselves either immoderately corrupt and ignorant or else overzealous adherents of reform. The former were the Eccentric heretics; the latter were the Reformists. One of the most striking Eccentrics of the early Middle Ages was Aldebert, a fanatic whom St. Boniface had difficulty in controlling. Aldebert claimed that he had been filled with grace while still in his mother's womb and that, a saint of God's election, he was born in a miraculous fashion. A charismatic personality, he preached to growing crowds of peasants and passed out his fingernail-parings and hair-cuttings as holy relics. He argued that his authority to preach derived from a letter which was written to him personally by Jesus and delivered by an angel. Boniface was not the man to take such disruptions of public order lightly, and he used every means at his disposal to combat them, including a number of synods and appeals to the pope for assistance. At last Aldebert disappeared, apparently less because of ecclesiastical pressures than because the people had tired of him.

Reformist dissenters were those who subscribed wholeheartedly to the reform of the Church but who, exposed to the ignorance and intolerance of the parish clergy, grew impatient and eventually radical in their demands. They perceived the contrast between the purity and simplicity of the apostolic Church and the decay of that of their own time, and they were impatient of any hesitation in returning to the Golden Age. Reformists had appeared in the eighth and ninth centuries—Claudius of Turin in Italy is an example—but they became more common and numerous in the eleventh, in response to the growing sentiment for reform throughout the Church. In 1025 a large band of Reformists was arrested and tried for heresy at Liège; Reformists were executed at Orléans in 1022; and from the 1020's on, there were numerous incidents throughout Europe, particularly in France, Germany, and the Low Countries.

Typically, Reformists began by attacking the immorality of the clergy. When improvement was slow in coming, they proceeded to attack the institution of the clergy in its entirety, arguing that men did not need mediators between themselves and God, that the true Church was invisible and consisted of those whom the Holy Spirit had illuminated. Their only authorities were the Bible and the inner light, and they rejected all that did not correspond to what the Holy Spirit told them was the interpretation of the Scriptures.

Exaggerations breed exaggerations; extremism on one side usually provokes extremism on the other. Both the established Church, in its search for order, and the Reformists, in their expression of prophecy, had exceeded moderation and upset the stability of the Church, which depended upon a salutary balance. The coldness and self-satisfaction of the established Church drove the Reformists into opposition; but opposition was precisely what was intolerable to the Church of order, which accordingly grew ever less tolerant of dissent. No one was executed for heresy in the Western Church between the sixth and the eleventh centuries, but beginning with the burning at Orléans in 1022, a new era of bloody intolerance began. Ironically, it was the desire to reform the Church that produced both the prophetic heresy and the orderly repression. The human tragedy of the situation was clearly demonstrated in a case at Cambrai in 1077. There a man named Ramihrd was arrested for preaching against the corruption of the clergy. The mob seized him from the bishop, took him out to the end of town, and burned him to death. Ramihrd's guilt consisted in preaching to an ignorant and conservative clergy at Cambrai the very moral doctrines then being advocated by the reforming pope in Rome.

Education and intellectual achievement were among the most important and durable programs of the reform movements. The efforts of Charlemagne, Charles the Bald, Alfred the Great, and the Ottos, combined with those of the monasteries, contributed to the growth of literacy and learning among both the clergy and the laity. The kings obtained much success in their program of education for social utility. Under Charlemagne, for example, the monks developed a style of writing called the Caroline minuscule, which was more legible than previous styles and became the model for our present lower-case letters. At the palace school, Alcuin formally established the seven arts of Boethius as the basis of education, dividing them into the trivium (grammar, rhetoric, and dialectic) and the quadrivium (arithmetic, geometry, music, and astronomy). The trivium and the quadrivium continued to be the core of undergraduate education throughout the Middle Ages and into the Renaissance, and they were the basis for the later development of more advanced subjects: the quadrivium promoted the study of mathematics and science; from grammar proceeded the humanistic study of literature; from rhetoric developed legal studies; and from dialectic came scholastic philosophy.

Yet in the period 700–1050 there were few original thinkers. The intellectual level of the seventh century was too low a base from which to start, and scholars had perforce to devote themselves to elementary education. Neither royal concern with social utility nor the excessive medieval reverence for the past promoted nonconformity. Carolingian culture was an attempt to revive and to combine the wisdom and glory of early Christianity, classical Rome, and royal Jerusalem. Charlemagne and his court even affected antique names: Charlemagne was David, Alcuin was Horace, and Theodulf, the poet and architect, was Pindar. As society and culture as a whole became more settled in the later tenth and early eleventh century, utilitarianism yielded enough to permit the rise of humanism, the study of the classics for their own sake. But this promoted pedantic imitation rather than originality.

The two most original thinkers of the period were Bede (673–735) and John Scotus Eriugena (c. 810–877). Bede was a monk at the abbey of Jarrow on the barren coast of Northumbria; and though he never journeyed more than a few miles from his birthplace, his genius made him the greatest scientist of the early Middle

Ages and the greatest historian since Augustine. He wrote on astronomy and cosmology, he calculated the tides for different latitudes and for different coastal configurations, and he popularized the dating from the birth of Christ that is now in use all over the world. But his most impressive work was his *Ecclesiastical History of the English Nation.*

This book is remarkable because it was the most critical and thoroughly investigated work of history since Thucydides. Although he himself remained at Jarrow, Bede interviewed visitors to the abbey, obtained whatever books were pertinent to his subject, and even sent out research assistants throughout England and as far as Rome to copy materials otherwise unavailable. Rising above the narrow parochialism of an era in which local churches or abbeys were the most usual subjects for the historian's pen and in which the English kingdoms were still politically disunited, he treated the history of the English people as a whole. Avoiding the rambling and logically inconsequent style of the chroniclers, Bede's history is tightly organized and structured on a theme: the gradual conversion of the English from paganism and from Irish Christianity to Roman Catholicism, which was to be the focus for the unity of the island. Bede is the only historian of the early Middle Ages who seems to have comprehended the great historical implications of Augustine's thought and who has worked out a story illustrating the meaningful and providentially purposive development of events. For Bede, history is not a jumbled box of moral maxims, but a dynamic development guided by the hand of God. Like Augustine, Bede used his great intellect to discern and to explicate the order both in the natural world and in human affairs.

Eriugena, an Irishman who settled at the court of Charles the Bald, where he taught and wrote philosophy, was strongly influenced by the mystical thought of Augustine, of the Neoplatonists, and of the Syrian monk Pseudo-Dionysius. For Eriugena, the true order of the universe is eternally veiled from man. "We do not know what God is...because He is infinite and therefore objectively unknowable. God Himself does not know what He is because He is not anything. Therefore, nothing can be predicated of God literally or affirmatively. Literally, God is not, because He transcends being."[1] This is not atheism; on the contrary, it is an affirmation that God's greatness transcends all human categories, even those of being and knowing. At the end of the world, "God, who is in Himself incomprehensible, will be somehow comprehended in the creature."[2]

[1]"The Division of Nature," trans. George B. Burch, in his *Early Medieval Philosophy* (New York, 1951), p. 11.
[2]*Ibid.*, p. 29.

Revolution

There were two varieties of reform in the Middle Ages, one motivated by prophecy and the other by order. The reform of order led to a program of political revolution in the eleventh and twelfth centuries which created a tightly knit ecclesiastical corporation under the leadership of the papacy. This revolution transformed the nature of the Church into a papal monarchy, and it made the papacy from 1050 to 1300 the single most important authority in western Europe.

The growth in the eleventh century of a more complex society made this revolution possible: expansion of the population and of the economy, extension of communications and increasing contacts with the world outside the West, the rise of the towns and of new social classes, the achievement of political stability, the size and efficiency of governments. In a simpler society, order could be obtained with a less rigid structure; now the diverse thrusts to nonconformity provoked from the forces of order a new and far more ambitious offensive. It was in the period after 1050 that the transformation of the Church from a community to a corporation was achieved.

The papalists used two primary arguments to justify the creation of a tightly organized Church under papal monarchy. The first emphasized the continuity between papalist reform and the earlier reform movements. Moral reform, the argument went, can only be accomplished when the influence of the laity is removed from the Church; and the influence of the laity can be removed only when the Church obtains enough political power to enforce its independence. The second argument was derived from natural law. It is necessary that human law be established in accordance with the principle of justice, that it be in accordance with the will of God. Any human law that is unjust must either be changed or considered null and void. Any ruler who does not rule according to the principles of justice must be corrected or deposed. But how are the Christian people to judge whether a law or a ruler is just? If every man decides for himself on the basis of his own conscience which laws he should obey, the result is anarchy. Some objective authority is needed to which to refer, and that logical authority is the vicar of Peter, to whom Christ entrusted the leadership of his flock.

In practice, assertion of these papalist principles required a double program: tighter and more efficient organization of the Church under papal leadership, and exercise of papal authority over temporal affairs. Both sides of the program were revolutionary.

The internal constitution of the Church had been from the second century traditionally episcopal. It was ruled by a *collegium* of bishops which represented the community of the apostles and wielded as a body the authority granted the apostles by Christ. The *collegium* was, however, never a formally constituted body, except when it met as an ecumenical council. The great patriarchs, as we have seen, gradually increased their power over that of the other bishops. Because of their political importance, Rome and Constantinople had emerged by the fifth century as the two most influential sees. This state of affairs was confirmed in the seventh century, when the other patriarchal sees—Alexandria, Antioch, and Jerusalem—all fell into the hands of the Moslems. Aided by the increasing weakness and isolation of the Byzantine emperor and by the support of the English and the French, the papacy extended its power throughout the West. In the meanwhile, it continued to exercise influence in the East as well, and even at Constantinople the pope was recognized as *primus inter pares* among the bishops.

The papal position, which had made such great strides in the eighth century, advanced rapidly in the period from the eleventh through the thirteenth, when the old tradition of a community of bishops was replaced by the idea of papal monarchy. The authority of Christ, instead of being delegated to the apostles as a whole, was now deemed to have been delegated to Peter, who then in turn delegated it to his apostolic colleagues. Hence the pope was the vicar of Christ on earth (this title now replaced that of "vicar of Peter"), and the bishops derived their authority from him. The result was the creation of a strongly organized Church under the monarchy of the pope, where the discipline and doctrine of the papacy could be everywhere enforced. As in the early Church the Mystical Body of Christ had been identified with the Christian community *(ecclesia)* and the Christian community with the institutional Church, so now the Church was identified with the *ecclesia romana.* The pope was the representative of, and the ultimate authority over, the entire Christian community. This was itself a revolutionary program.

But the papalists' attitude toward the temporal power was even more revolutionary. There were three broad theories of the relationship of the temporal to the spiritual power current in the Middle Ages. All assumed, as almost all societies have until recent times, that there was no distinction between Church and State. Indeed, such a distinction would have appeared meaningless. The Church, like the State, was responsible for the order of society; the State, like the Church, was responsible for promoting the salvation of its members. Each was a manifestation of a united Christian society. Of the three fundamental ways in which authority over Christian society could be conceived, the first placed the emperor at its head, with authority passing from God to the emperor, who delegated temporal authority to the kings and princes and spiritual authority to the pope and bishops. The second theory argued parallelism: Christ granted spiritual authority directly to the pope and temporal authority directly to the emperor. Parallelism was a nice compromise, but uncongenial to the medieval desire for a simple cosmos. In the third theory the pope was at the head and, receiving his powers directly from Christ, delegated spiritual authority to bishops, councils, and abbots and temporal authority to the emperor and kings.

From the time of Constantine through that of Henry III of Germany (1039–1056), who deposed three popes, the imperial theory generally prevailed in practice, for the simple reason that imperial power was usually much greater than papal power. On occasion a strong pope like Nicholas I (858–867) would assert the superiority of the spiritual to the temporal, but until 1048 such papal boldness was exceptional.

After the election of Leo IX in 1048, the papal position grew rapidly more powerful until, following a long conflict with the temporal rulers, the popes emerged victorious. From about 1125 to about 1300 it was the papalist theory of Christian society that generally prevailed over the imperial. An enormous revolution had been accomplished.

The papal revolution was what sociologists call "norm-oriented": that is, it accepted traditional assumptions about society, simply replacing one supreme ruler of that society—the emperor—with another—the pope. It was not "value-oriented": it did not challenge the fundamental structure of society. The analogy is closer to the American among modern revolutions than to the French or Russian. There was enough corruption in the eleventh-century Church, and enough enthusiasm for more sweeping reforms, that in retrospect a more fundamental revolution would seem to have been possible, like the one that eventually did occur with the Protestant Reformation in the sixteenth century. But medieval society was too conservative and not yet complex enough socially to support such a violent change. Furthermore, the papacy proved successful in capturing the reform movement by setting itself at its head. In the history of the Catholic Church there have been three periods of acute crisis: the eleventh century, the sixteenth, and the twentieth. In the sixteenth century the papacy failed to align itself with the forces of reform until it was too late, the result being the Protestant Reformation; it is not yet clear whether the papacy of the twentieth century is able or willing to meet the challenge of reform; but in the eleventh century a succession of able and devoted popes, by assuming the leadership of reform themselves, diverted the currents of revolution from radical into essentially moderate channels.

The dispute around which the revolution centered, according to most medieval writers as well as many historians, was over investitures. The investiture controversy concerned the propriety of a lay ruler's bestowing upon a bishop the symbols of his spiritual rule. Investiture was the feudal ceremony in which a lord gave his vassal a kernel of wheat, a clod of earth, or some other symbol of the fief that the vassal was receiving in return for his homage. Since so many bishops were themselves feudal vassals, they received investiture for their fiefs from their lords, usually the kings. The kings, who were accustomed to appoint the bishops, acquired the additional habit not only of investing them with the symbols of their spiritual power, but also of bestowing upon them the episcopal ring and crozier (pastoral staff), symbols of their spiritual authority. To the papal reformers, there could be no clearer symbol of what they considered the fundamental difficulty with the Church: lay influence.

But the issue of lay investiture was for the most part only symbolic. Directly underlying it was a more important issue: who had the right to appoint the bishop? In the early Church, bishops were elected by the united acclamation of the clergy and people. In the more formalized Church of the Middle Ages, such spontaneity was exceptional, and it became general practice for the cathedral chapter to act as representatives of the clergy and people of the diocese in the election of a bishop. As royal intervention increased, it became even more common for the kings simply to appoint the candidate. Election did not permit a bishop to enter immediately upon his duties; he had first to be consecrated—to receive the laying on of hands by other bishops—before he was considered to have apostolic succession. But this presented little difficulty to the kings, who could always procure from among

117

their loyal episcopal supporters the three bishops requisite for consecration. It was this royally appointed episcopate with its temporal loyalties that the papal reformers were most interested in
suppressing and replacing with papally nominated bishops. It seems
to have seldom occurred to the reformers that it was hopeless to
try to remove lay interference in the Church as long as the Church
wielded political influence.

Underlying the dispute over episcopal elections was a deeper
struggle that some historians have classified as a warfare between
Church and State. This classification is insufficient. In the first
place, few people at the time would have understood the distinction between Church and State, and it is always tricky to argue
that people are really fighting for something different from what
they believe they are fighting for. In the second place, the phrase
"Church versus State" conjures up a picture in which popes, monks,
and bishops on the one side confront emperors, kings, and nobles
on the other. Nothing could be farther from the truth. At the
height of the war between the Emperor Henry IV and Pope
Gregory VII, the majority of the German bishops, as was quite
natural for royal appointees, supported the emperor. On the other
hand, the chief allies of the pope were many of the German nobility, who for their own political purposes wished to weaken the
imperial position. Many of the monks were prophetically indifferent to the question of who should dominate the Christian order;
they were, on the whole, inclined to accept the royal domination
of the Church and to regard papalism as unnecessary and irrelevant to the true spiritual demands of Christianity. The situation
by 1080, when Gregory VII had chosen a king of his own and
Henry IV his own pope, demonstrates the inadequacy of the
"Church versus State" interpretation. On one side was a pope, a
king aspiring to be emperor, bishops, abbots, princes, knights, and
townspeople; on the other side was an emperor, a pope, bishops,
abbots, princes, knights, and townspeople.

The struggle is therefore best understood as a vast civil war
affecting all segments of a united and indivisible Christian society.
The revolution consisted in the success of the popes in substituting

themselves for the emperor as the supreme authority in that society.

The papal revolution began in 1048 with the election of Leo IX, but, like most revolutions, it had been prepared for by the previous development of a revolutionary theory. The papalists claimed Petrine texts of the Gospels as the source of their position, contending that Christ's commission to Peter is nowhere matched by any corresponding commission to Caesar or any secular power. They referred also to the words of Gelasius I to the Emperor Anastasius I in 494: "There are two chief powers ruling this world: the holy authority of the popes [*auctoritas*] and the royal power [*potestas*]. The spiritual power is more important than the temporal because it is responsible to God for the kings themselves." Gelasius' meaning was not clear, but the papalists chose the interpretation pleasing to them, that *auctoritas* is superior to *potestas* and that the kings are responsible to the spiritual power.

In the eighth and ninth centuries, papalist arguments were advanced by the Donation of Constantine and by other forgeries. In the first half of the ninth century a number of documents were forged in the episcopal chanceries of northern France. Purporting to be collections of early papal and conciliar decrees, the forgeries were a clever mingling of real and spurious materials, with the aim of showing that in the ancient tradition of the Church the kings did not intervene in its affairs. The false decretals, as they were called, built up the prestige of the bishops and, incidentally, that of the pope, whom, as a more distant authority, they preferred to the king. The great Pope Nicholas I (858–867), taking advantage of temporary royal weakness, further advanced papalist theory. In the first place, Nicholas argued, the papacy receives its rights directly from God, and the "foremost see is therefore to be judged by no one" (*Prima sedes non judicabitur a quoquam*). Bishops, councils, kings and emperors, all these derive their powers from the pope, who is the protector of the whole Christian people in matters of discipline and doctrine.

In the tenth and eleventh centuries, two great prelates from

Liège, ironically one of the centers of reform theory as well as one of the strongholds of imperial politics, urged the superiority of the spiritual to the temporal power. Rather (d. 974), bishop of Liège and then of Verona, argued the supremacy of the episcopacy in general, without special reference to the pope. "Bishops," Rather declared in one of his less temperate moods, "are gods, lords, messiahs, angels, patriarchs, prophets, apostles, martyrs, anointed kings, princes, judges...." Wazo, bishop of Liège from 1042 to 1048, defied the Emperor Henry III (1039–1056) on three occasions, declaring: "...to you we owe fidelity; but to the pope we owe obedience. To you, O king, we must answer for worldly things; to the pope, however, we must answer for everything concerning God's service."

With these ideas current, particularly in northern Italy and Lorraine, only the opportunity was needed in order to launch a revolutionary program. That opportunity was provided by Henry III at the synod of Sutri (1046). Henry III was a pious emperor, who believed that it was the emperor's duty to control the Church and to direct it toward morality and Christian purity. He believed that his authority entitled him to depose and appoint popes according to his best judgment; and he was the last emperor effectively to exercise this power. In 1046 there were three claimants to the papal throne: Benedict IX, whom the chroniclers describe as "bestial," the representative of one noble Roman family; Sylvester III, the almost equally reprehensible candidate of another family; and Gregory VI, a generally reputable and moral man who, however, was guilty of simony in purchasing the papacy from Benedict IX. To straighten out a situation that was spiritually unedifying and conducive to political instability, Henry III intervened, and at two synods in December, 1046 (Sutri, December 20, and Rome, December 23), he secured the resignation of, or deposed, all three candidates. Gregory VI went north to Lorraine in exile, accompanied by his relative Hildebrand. Henry proceeded to appoint as pope two German bishops in succession, Clement II (1046–1047) and Damasus II (1048), both of whom pursued policies of reform under imperial patronage. On the death of Damasus, Henry appointed yet another German bishop, Bruno of Toul, whom he confidently expected to continue the policies of his predecessors.

Bruno, who took the throne name of Leo IX (1048–1054), did not disappoint Henry in his devotion to the cause of reform; but he was from Lorraine and had learned the papalist rhetoric of that region. When he came down to Rome as pope he brought with him a brain trust of papalist Lorrainers: Humbert, whom Leo made cardinal bishop of Silva Candida; Frederick, the brother of Duke Godfrey of Lorraine; Hugh the White; and Hildebrand, who, though an Italian, had spent two years in the north with Gregory VI. Leo was unwilling to make a radical break with the emperor, whose good will he desired and upon whom he relied for support against the Normans of southern Italy; but he did undertake an unprecedented tour of France and Germany, calling reform synods, visiting dioceses, and building up in northern Europe a more direct consciousness of the presence and prerogatives of Rome, with the hope of bringing the bishops under papal rather than imperial control.

Leo's successor was Victor II (1054–1057), who worked closely with the emperor, but imperial influence was badly shaken by the death of Henry III in 1056. Henry was succeeded by his six-year-old son, Henry IV, under the regency of his wife, the Empress Agnes, a pious and trusting but by no means a politically astute woman. The next year, Victor II died and was succeeded by Frederick of Lorraine, who took the title Stephen IX (1057–1058). Stephen's family was violently anti-imperial, and the new pope not only neglected to notify the regent of his election, but even entertained the idea of placing his own brother, Duke Godfrey, on the imperial throne. The erosion of the imperial position vis-à-vis the papacy now became marked. It was the result not so much of any weakening of imperialist theory, but of the practical disadvantages of a weak and indecisive regency.

It was under these conditions that Humbert of Silva Candida was encouraged to publish a work that he had completed earlier but had feared to publish while Henry III was still alive. This was the *Three Books against the Simoniacs,* the opening shot in a long battle of the books between papalist and imperialist theoreticians. Humbert's position was that the root of evil was lay influence in the Church and that there could be no effective reform unless this were wholly rooted out. The entire function of the temporal power was to act as the arm of the Church, of which the pope was the head: the emperor and the kings existed for the sole purpose of protecting the clergy and of executing their orders. The Mystical Body of Christ is identified with the bishop of Rome and his cardinals: the pope is to society as the sun is to the universe; the emperor is like the pale moon, shining only with reflected light. These ideas, the most radical statement to date of the papalist position, were put into practice by subsequent popes.

After a short interlude following the death of Stephen IX, the revolution passed out of the hands of the Lorrainers into the hands of Italian reformers who were no less radical. Gerard, the archbishop of Florence, who became Nicholas II (1059–1061), launched two effective attacks upon the lay power. In 1059 at a great synod in Rome at the Lateran palace, where the medieval popes dwelt, Nicholas issued the first formal prohibition of lay investiture and the first formal regulation concerning the election of the pope. Henceforth, in order to prevent further imperial interference, the pope was to be elected by the cardinals of the Roman Church, and all lay interference was strictly forbidden. Later, at the Council of Lyon in 1274, it was decreed that the cardinals meet in conclave (*con clave*: locked up "with a key") so as to preserve absolute secrecy and freedom from attempts to influence the election from outside.

All the reform popes till now had had short reigns, and only the debility of the empress's politics had enabled them to get away with so much. But Nicholas II was followed by two popes in succession, both Italians, both as vigorous as any of their predecessors, and both enjoying long tenure in office: Alexander II (1061–1073) and the famous Hildebrand, who took the throne name of Gregory VII (1073–1085). It was under these two popes that the theories of papal supremacy were first put into wide practice; the reign of Gregory VII, in particular, made it clear that the struggle for the control of Christian society was joined to the death. Hildebrand was born in Italy, was for a short time a monk, and then, as a relative and friend of Pope Gregory VI, learned something of papal politics, including their disappointments. After accompanying Gregory into exile, he returned to Rome with Leo IX as a member of the brain trust and rose rapidly in the ranks of the hierarchy as subdeacon, legate, and eventually (1059) archdeacon. As archdeacon, he exercised almost as much power as the pope himself; and the monk Peter Damian, whose prophetic spirit did not allow him to be impressed with the claims of spiritual order, cynically suggested that "if you want to live in Rome, you have to declare loudly that you follow the pope's lord more than the lord pope." In 1073, he was finally elected pope in violation of the Lateran Decree of 1059, by acclamation of the people. Called by his German friends Hellbrand ("Bright Flame") and by his enemies Höllebrand ("Hellfire"), Gregory's life is proof that a burning spirit can dwell within a breast committed to order. He was convinced that he had a divine mission to reform society and that his power over society was, under God, unlimited. No longer merely the vicar of Peter but now the vicar of Christ, the pope has, he argued, the duty of exercising his authority over all the earth.

Three conditions prepared the way for the implementation of Gregory's program: the weakness of the empire, the tradition, now twenty-five years old, of the revolutionary papacy, and the development of canon law. It was from a perusal of the old decrees of canon law, both legitimate and forged, that the famous *Dictatus Papae* was compiled. This curious document, which was placed in the official register about 1075, is an unorganized list of the titles of a collection of real or supposititious canons from the past, compiled by Gregory or one of his supporters in support of papalism. It contains some memorable statements: only the Roman pontiff is rightly called universal; he alone can depose or reestablish bishops; he alone can use imperial insignia; all princes must kiss his feet; he is entitled to depose kings.

The practical program of Alexander II and Gregory VII was almost as impressive as their theoretical statements: to reform and reorganize the Church, to establish papal authority in the Eastern Church, to reclaim Spain for Christianity, and in all this to enlist the support and obedience of the kings of the West.

The papal policy in regard to the internal organization of the Church resulted in its being transformed into a papal monarchy. The means used were these. First, papal government at Rome was strengthened and expanded. The *curia,* the equivalent of the *consilium* (administrative and advisory council) of the kings, grew larger and complex. The *curia* was dominated by the cardinals, who, together with the pope, formed the *ecclesia romana,* which was in turn identified with the whole Christian community. Cardinals originally existed in many dioceses and were so called because they were "hinges" *(cardines)* between two churches: a cardinal priest would have a parish but also be invited to serve as an administrator in the cathedral. Gradually, particularly in Rome, where the task of administration was great, the cardinals came to lose all but a nominal connection with their original parishes. Certain parishes in Rome came to be established as cardinals' parishes with only nominal duties, and to these the popes would appoint those whom they wished to have as administrators. Certain deaconries in Rome and certain tiny dioceses around Rome were also set aside for administrative purposes, so that there were cardinal-bishops and cardinal-deacons as well as cardinal-priests. The power of the cardinals in the administration has been so great that they have ever since been under attack.

With the growth of the papal administration came an enormous increase in the volume of papal correspondence: regulating jurisdictional disputes and protecting legitimate bishops and monasteries against usurpers, admonishing recalcitrant bishops, upbraiding meddlesome rulers, and urging bishops and synods to take stronger measures for reform. Another means of papal control was the summoning of councils and the encouragement of local councils or synods. No ecumenical council had been called since the ninth century, for the imperial power was weak, and the papacy did not yet feel itself in a strong enough position to dominate one. But from the time of Nicholas II the popes called frequent and ever-larger synods, until in 1123 the First Lateran Council began a series of ecumenical assemblies summoned by the popes and directed to enact papal policies.

Among the popes' most effective weapons were the legates. A legate was an officer sent out to a locality by the papal court with full jurisdiction over a particular problem just as if he were pope. For example, Alexander II sent Peter Damian with full papal powers as a legate to Germany in 1069 to persuade the young King Henry IV not to divorce his wife. But under Gregory VII and his successors, such temporary legatine missions were often supplemented by sending out legates with long terms of office and with jurisdiction over wide areas. For example, Gregory sent Hugh of Die to France with the authority to act throughout that kingdom exactly as if he were the pope himself. Hugh was fanatically loyal to Rome and, more Catholic than the pope, he believed wholeheartedly that only unbending adherence to papal decrees could be tolerated and that harshness was the only way to keep the Church in line. Wherever he went, he took precedence over the local bishops and archbishops; he visited dioceses and parishes demanding moral reform; he called synods and councils on his own authority; and he even deposed bishops—including, in 1080, the powerful Manasses of Reims, who had with some asperity refused to attend a council to which he was summoned by the legate.

In consequence of these extensions of papal power, the authority of bishops and local synods gradually deteriorated. From a loosely organized Christian community, the Church became a papal monarchy. One result was that the lay authorities were now confronted with a Church that was more tightly organized than ever and more difficult for them to control. On the other hand, far from relinquishing its political power in the name of reform, the Church acquired more, and the need of the kings to dominate it was therefore increased rather than diluted. Under these conditions, conflict became inevitable.

The struggle of the papacy with the empire was not limited to the Western empire. As early as the reign of Leo IX, the reform popes were determined to restore their authority in the East, which had been deteriorating for centuries as the doctrines and practices of the two halves of the Christian Church drifted slowly apart. In 1054, Leo sent the two firebrands Frederick of Lorraine and Humbert of Silva Candida to Constantinople to work out an agreement with Emperor Constantine IX. Constantine was willing, but the patriarch of Constantinople, Michael Kerullarios, who matched Humbert in intolerance and rashness, deliberately humiliated the papal legates and provoked the mob to outrages against churches of the Latin rite. Kerullarios was determined to end papal influence at Constantinople, once and for all, and he succeeded in provoking the legates to take actions that equalled his own rashness: they formally laid upon the high altar of the Cathedral of Hagia Sophia a bull excommunicating him. The emperor tried in vain to bring the antagonists to a conference table. Kerullarios publicly burned the papal bull, and the legates went home to urge a policy of harshness and coercion against the East. The events of 1054 are the most dramatic in the long process of division between the Roman

Catholic and the Eastern Orthodox Churches, and they were confirmed by the bloody wars of the Western crusaders in the East. Only in the second half of the twentieth century has any progress been made in restoring relations. If the meeting of Pope Paul VI and the Patriarch Athenagoras of Constantinople in Jerusalem in 1965 and the formal lifting of the excommunication of Michael Kerullarios that same year did not shake the world with their daring, they at least symbolize a spirit of compromise that for nine hundred years has not been much in evidence.

The papal zeal for the assimilation of the Eastern Church extended to the conversion of Jews, heretics, and Moslems as well, and it was Gregory VII who first contemplated calling Christians to arms to liberate the Holy Land. This crusading ideal, which would be further developed by the popes of the twelfth and thirteenth centuries, seems an ironic manifestation of a religion founded by the Prince of Peace. Yet it was a logical—if not a reasonable—corollary of papalist theory. If the pope was indeed the vicegerent of Christ over Christian society and consequently over the world, he had a true authority to enforce on the world the demands of Christian morality and the edicts of Christian law. Enforcement of law logically entails, and has historically always included, the use of force. Hence the pressures put on the Eastern Church, hence the increased prosecution of heretics, hence the growing intolerance of Jews, hence the crusading spirit and the eventual foundation of military-oriented religious orders like the Templars, and hence the approval of civil war and rebellion as measures against the disobedient kings and emperors of the West.

Because the papacy was situated in the West, it was in the West that the conflict with the temporal powers was most violent. The papalist attitude toward the kings of France and England was often as severe as that toward the Western emperor, but because it was the emperor in whose domains Rome lay and because it was the emperor who, like the pope, claimed authority over all Christian society, it was against the empire that the papacy exerted its most vigorous efforts.

In 1066 Henry IV (1056–1106), having reached the age of sixteen, began his personal rule. The young king inherited the determination and political skill but not the favorable political circumstances of his father, for the ten-year regency of his mother had reduced royal power in relation both to the Church and to the nobility. Henry immediately turned his energies toward restoring it to its former heights. Since the bishops still possessed great political influence, it was absolutely necessary to control them if political order was to be reestablished. In 1073 Gregory VII came to the papal throne, possessed of determination and energy equal to Henry's, and equally resolved to control the bishops.

From 1073 to 1076 an uneasy peace prevailed between the two men: they wrote letters expressing their mutual esteem, and Gregory supported Henry in his successful repression of a major rebellion in Saxony from 1073 to 1075. But the *Dictatus Papae* of 1075 already indicated that Gregory would not tolerate the reestablishment of imperial domination of the Church, and in the same year the pope issued a formal decree against the investiture of bishops by laymen. When early in 1076 dispute over the succession to the archdiocese of Milan made it clear that emperor and pope were going to press irreconcilable claims to name bishops, the battle was joined. By the end of February, 1076, each had threatened the other with deposition. By autumn, events in Germany gave the advantage to the pope. The nobles of southern Germany rebelled against the king, whose growing power they feared, and they met at Tribur in October to seek an alliance with the pope.

In order to avert what would have been a deadly combination Henry crossed the Alps and in January, 1077, waited on the pope for three days outside the castle of Canossa, where Gregory was in residence, begging him for forgiveness. It was a humiliation from which Henry reaped considerable short-term advantages. Gregory, reluctantly weighing the duties of Christian charity more heavily than those of political expedience, granted absolution to the king in return for Henry's promise that he would allow the pope to judge between him and the rebellious nobles. The nobility went ahead and at Forchheim in 1077 declared the king deposed, electing Rudolf of Swabia in his place. Gregory, abiding by the agreement of Canossa, refused to sanction this action on the grounds that Henry would remain the rightful ruler until he was properly judged by the pope. Thus Henry shrewdly and at the cost only of temporary humiliation broke the papal alliance with the nobles. He returned to Germany and waged successful war against his opponents, while Gregory kept his own counsel and declared for neither side. In 1080, at last convinced of Henry's bad faith, Gregory declared the king deposed "for his insolence, disobedience and deceit" and recognized Rudolf as the rightful ruler. It was a dramatic moment in the history of the Church: on several occasions emperors had deposed popes, but never before had a pope presumed to depose an emperor. But it was too late. In the same year Henry called his own synod to depose Gregory as a false monk, sorcerer, fornicator, and plotter of murder. Rudolf died in the fall, and though another pretender was elected, Gregory's German allies were in disorder and shortly ended effective resistance. With his military supremacy, Henry was able to capture Rome by 1084, install his own pope, and drive Gregory to die in exile in 1085.

In the meanwhile, the conflict of theories was as violent as that of armies. The manifestos of Humbert and his colleagues elicited response from imperialist writers. Sigebert of Gembloux accused the papacy of fostering Reformist heresy by pressing its program of reform, an accusation curiously like that made by modern Catholic conservatives against progressives. The accusation was justified, for once an institution encourages a spirit of reform and change, there will inevitably be those who are disappointed that change is not proceeding fast enough and who move from moderate to radical discontent. But it is also true that without persistent reform, an institution will cease to respond to the needs of society and ultimately wither away. The imperialists argued, correctly, that they were conserving the ancient tradition of the

Church and that the papalists were innovators, a charge that in the conservative Middle Ages the papacy was concerned to deny. But had innovations not been made, there would have occurred either a violent revolution like the sixteenth-century Reformation or else a gradual dissolution and decay of Christianity such as has taken place in the twentieth century.

As the papalist theoreticians advanced their position, and as the political power of the emperor weakened, the imperialist theoreticians faltered. Peter Crassus, a lawyer from Ravenna and a friend both of Henry IV and of the antipope set up by the king, wrote a treatise *In Defense of King Henry.* He used the precedents of Roman law to deny the pope's right to excommunicate the king and to revive the argument that the king had the right to order all aspects of society in his kingdom. But Peter's arguments betray an unintentional retreat from the imperialist argument that there must be a unified Christian society under the rule of the emperor. For he speaks of two orders of men, one bound by canon law and the other by secular law, implying parallelism rather than imperial supremacy. What had happened was this: before the eleventh century, the imperial theory of Christian society was dominant, so that often the anti-imperialists, like Wazo of Liège, merely demanded parallelism. But when the papalist position hardened and claimed supremacy for itself, the imperialists retreated defensively into parallelism. Another ambivalence of Peter is that he seems to be defending not the rights of one emperor over all society, but the rights of each king in his own kingdom, a step toward the recognition of a political and ecclesiastical pluralism previously unheard of in the Middle Ages.

A writer known as the Norman Anonymous pursued these royalist arguments deliberately. Accepting the unity of Christian society, he nevertheless argued that its leadership was in the hands of the kings. Christ, he said, appears in the Gospels more as a king than as a priest, and it is therefore the kings who most directly represent Christ. As for ecclesiastical government itself, papalism is a fraud, for apostolic authority lies with the bishops as a whole, not with the successor of Peter.

Thus the anti-papalist writers moved insensibly away from imperialism toward new positions which would be developed further in the later Middle Ages. The most important of these are political pluralism, the first intimations of nationalism; and conciliarism, resistance to papal monarchy in the name of episcopal collegiality.

The papalist writers of the twelfth century also made some interesting departures from the hierocratic ideas of the past. Honorius of Canterbury argued that the pope had direct authority over the clergy and indirect authority over the kings. But he equated neither clergy nor kings with the *ecclesia,* which was, rather, the "people of God." John of Salisbury (1110–1180) pressed the identification of *populus* and *ecclesia* even farther. The king must rule in accordance with justice; if he does not, he becomes a "tyrant," and the people may disobey his laws, depose him, or even kill him. John is still a papalist, and he insists that the pope must approve such action to make it legitimate, but the principle that all policies must be judged by their effects upon the welfare of the people and that the people are at least in part the judge of these policies was a departure from tradition in the direction of popular authority. In the fourteenth century Marsilius of Padua would further develop this notion of popular authority and social contract, and from there the theory would grow until it reached Locke, Rousseau, and Jefferson. Without fully understanding the implications of their arguments, both the papalist and the imperialist writers were encouraging the growth of the "ascending theory"[1] of sovereignty, which argues that God does not delegate his authority downwards through pope or emperor but upwards through the people. Kings, popes, bishops, and emperors then possess their authority as a trust from the people whose representatives they are. But this notion was far from explicit, let alone prevalent, in the conflicts of the late eleventh and early twelfth centuries, when "descending" theories, either papal or imperial, still held sway.

[1]See Walter Ullmann, *Principles of Government and Politics in the Middle Ages* (New York, 1961).

131

Those conflicts were not resolved until after the end of the eleventh century. The victory of Henry IV over Gregory VII was not conclusive. Urban II (1088–1099) and Paschal II (1099–1118) continued the war against Henry and his antipope, and by 1104 the papacy had again built a powerful coalition of German nobles, led by Henry's son (soon to be Henry V) against the old emperor. These events did not escape the attention of the chroniclers as a perfect text for the vanity of vanities and the contempt of the world. Even as Henry IV and his antipope, Clement III, had driven Gregory VII to die in exile, so now Henry V and Paschal II drove Henry IV to die in Liège, the last city in his dominions to remain loyal to him.

If Paschal hoped that Henry V (1106–1125) would be more agreeable to papal claims than his father, he was mistaken. No vigorous emperor could afford to tolerate papal domination of his clergy. The new king resumed royal efforts to control the bishops; Paschal renewed the excommunication of anyone granting lay investiture; and after an inconclusive interview between the two in 1111, the emperor seized the pope and threw him into a dungeon. There he remained without food until he acquiesced in the imperial demands, which he of course denounced once he was well free of Henry's grasp. Under Paschal and Calixtus II (1119–1124), a number of agreements were worked out with the kings of France, Germany, and England regarding investitures—agreements which were essentially compromises beneficial to the kings. The kings agreed to invest the bishops only with the symbols of their temporal possessions and to leave the investment with the ring and crozier to the ecclesiastical authorities. But the kings were to invest with the temporals *before* consecration, an arrangement leaving the king a veto over the election of the bishop which was much more important than the settlement of the symbolic issue. This compromise on investitures therefore had little bearing upon the struggle, which continued unabated.

The ultimate victory of the papacy in Germany was achieved not by negotiations nor by the triumph of a theory, but by a shift in dynastic politics. Henry V died in 1125 leaving no direct heir, and the title passed to his distant cousin Lothar II of Saxony (1125–1137). Lothar was a member of the Welf dynasty, one of the princely families that had long supported the papacy against the emperor. This tradition, in addition to the more important fact that Lothar's weak and disputed claim to the throne obliged him to make concessions to the Church in order to secure its support, meant the end of effective imperial opposition to the papacy. The increasing weakness of the German monarchy now allowed the papacy to press in wherever the empire retreated. The bishops drifted away from imperial control, either to return to their old independence or to support the papacy. Papal appointments to episcopal sees now became common for the first time.

The papal revolution was well under way by the 1130's. The popes had been successful in establishing hierarchical order within the Church and in dislodging imperialist claims to supremacy over Christian society in favor of their own. From that time until 1300 would be the only period in medieval history in which the papacy really dominated society. It remained for the popes of the twelfth and thirteenth centuries to develop and expand their position. Yet already, by the beginning of the twelfth century, the seeds of future discontents were visible to a discerning eye. The decline of imperial power and the growth, both in practice and in theory, of political pluralism presaged the rise of the national monarchies, which would after 1300 bring down both papacy and empire, and shatter the ideal of the unified Christian society. And the prophetic elements in the Church were increasingly dissatisfied with a Church that the principles of order were making more rigid, more temporally involved, and less responsive to the expression of the direct religious experience.

ix The Thrust of the Prophetic Spirit

Enthusiasm for reform in the eleventh and twelfth centuries encouraged the prophetic spirit as well as the spirit of order. Indeed, the more the forces of order transformed the Church into a formalized and corporate organization, the more did religiously enthusiastic people seek elsewhere for fulfillment. The powerful thrust of the prophetic spirit is thus the result not only of popular enthusiasm for reform in general but of rebellion against the advance of the spirit of order. This rebellion expressed itself in movements of popular piety, in new monastic orders, in mysticism, and in new movements of heresy.

The formalization of the Christian liturgy and sacraments, which had been well under way by the eighth century, continued into the eleventh. The Western Church had always been more legalistic than the Eastern; and with the development of canon law and the vast extension of ecclesiastical organization under the papacy, with its councils, its decrees, its legatine commissions, and its curia and cardinals, legalism advanced even further. The Mass still lacked meaning for most people, and the sacraments were often received, as the laws of the Church were accepted, without real understanding. Participation in religion was often limited to formal and external observances.

In the face of this advancing formalism came the great upsurge of religious enthusiasm in the eleventh and twelfth centuries, an upsurge attributable in part to the continuation and maturation of the earlier reform movements and in part, possibly, to the dislocation of society by the sudden economic and social changes attendant upon the rapid rise of population.

Great numbers of all classes, then, wished to express their religious enthusiasm in ways that seemed more personally satisfying than those provided by the formalized Church. The result was the growth of pious practices whose purpose was to bring the individual into a more direct religious experience. Anything was embraced that rendered the spiritual sphere closer and more attainable: hence the fervent practice of the cult of saints, especially veneration for their relics and for places physically connected with them. It was thought that the physical remains of a holy person retained some of his sacred power, and every church strove to acquire a skull, a tooth, or at least a fragment of a venerable thighbone. These relics were sometimes placed under the cornerstone of the altar and sometimes set into ornaments of exquisite design known as reliquaries. The relic was often the focal point for visitors to the church, who made their vows to the saint or offered him gifts in return for, or in hope of, services rendered.

Certain shrines, renowned for the special piety of their saints or the miraculous circumstances surrounding their origins, became centers of long pilgrimages. The alleged burial place in Spain of the Apostle James, revealed to a monk by a miraculous star, became the shrine of Santiago de Compostella, visited by pilgrims from all over the West. The shrine of Our Lady of Chartres, that of St. Thomas Becket at Canterbury, that of St. Peter at Rome, and, most important, that of the Holy Sepulchre in Jerusalem, the traditional tomb of Christ, were visited by pilgrims whose numbers and enthusiasm increased throughout the eleventh and succeeding centuries. In April, when the weather began to warm, "thanne longen folk to goon on pilgrimages,/

and palmeres for to seken straunge strondes,/to ferne halwes, kowthe in sondry londes...." [1] The pilgrimage was often a long and difficult task, but it could be undertaken by individuals as an act of deeply felt devotion. That men and women, many of them wealthy people of substance, should undertake journeys, under the most uncomfortable traveling conditions, that often endured for months or even years is proof of the fervent spirit of the time.

Of the saints, the most popular was the Blessed Virgin. The cult of the Virgin, though ancient in its origins, took a central place in Catholic worship only during this period. The Virgin was venerated in the first centuries of the Church but apparently to no greater degree than the most important apostles or Church fathers. The highly emotional defense of her title as Mother of God against the Nestorians in the fourth century suggests that by then she was already the center of special veneration—a veneration encouraged by the iconography of the Nativity, which invariably showed the baby God protected by his Mother. The cult of the Virgin was perhaps strongest in the East, but by the ninth century it was already deep-seated in the West as well. By that period Mary was already the mediator between man and God, praying mercifully to her Son for the sinner. As Christ was the new Adam, so Mary was the new Eve, who brought forth salvation on the earth as the old Eve had brought forth ruin. Born without sin, ever virgin, and sinless in her life, she was at once the ideal of maidenly purity and maternal devotion.

By the twelfth century the veneration of the Virgin had exceeded all previous limits and surpassed the boundaries of ecclesiastically approved doctrine. In a rough society that did little to protect him, the individual turned to this mother-sister figure with fervent devotion. Everywhere the Virgin worked miracles; everywhere she succored the poor, the sick, and the lonely. To anyone who showed her special devotion, she extended her special protection, and she more than once rescued a murderer from the

[1] "Then people long to go on pilgrimages, and palmers to seek strange shores and distant shrines known in many lands."

gallows because he had showed himself her special man. Devotion to Mary often descended into sentimentality, as in the famous tale of the "Juggler of Our Lady," where the little monk who is unable to write or paint or sing goes before the statue of the Virgin at night when all the other brothers are in bed and wins her special favor by juggling for her.

The doctrine of the Church ordinarily grows out of the meditations of theologians or the decisions of councils, but the special veneration of Mary was assimilated into Christian doctrine from popular devotion. It is a manifestation of the desire to humanize religion that transformed the representations of Christ in sculpture and painting from the stiff and hieratic judge of the universe to the suffering and wholly human victim, rejected and unjustly condemned by his fellow men. Mary was a kind and loving mother; she knew what it was like to feel bereavement and loss, and she could sympathize with the sufferings of poor mortals. The greatest hymn to the Virgin is perhaps the "Stabat Mater," written in the thirteenth century, which dwells upon her share in the tears of humanity:

> *Stabat mater dolorosa*
> *Iuxta crucem lachrymosa*
> *Dum pendebat filius;*
> *Cuius animam gementem*
> *Contristantem et dolentem*
> *Pertransivit gladius.*[2]

The wide extent of the Virgin's cult is reflected in the fact that of the cathedrals and churches erected in the twelfth and thirteenth centuries, an enormous proportion were dedicated to her. Most of the great cathedrals of France, for example, are cathedrals of Notre Dame: Notre Dame de Paris, Notre Dame de Chartres, Notre Dame d'Amiens, and so on. The erection of cathedrals all over Europe is in itself a manifestation of popular spiritual en-

[2]Weeping, the sorrowful Mother stood by the Cross while her Son hung dying. A sword had pierced her mourning and grieving soul that suffered with her Son.

thusiasm, for the enormous cost in money and in time was met in large part by the free donation of skills by artisans, architects, sculptors, and glaziers, and of hard labor or money by the population as a whole.

Popular enthusiasm also created a number of semimonastic movements like the Beghards and Beguines, laymen and women who lived a communal life dedicated to simplicity, poverty, and meditation. A similar enthusiasm brought about a revival of monasticism. The old reformed monasteries like that of Cluny or of Gorze had themselves been corrupted, and by the end of the eleventh century new reforms were necessary. But these new reforms were of a different nature from the old. The Benedictine order had ceased to be the center of educational, medical, and charitable activities. A more complex society demanded more advanced and specialized training in medicine and law, as well as in philosophy and theology, and this new training was best provided in the cities by the episcopal schools and later by the universities that arose from the episcopal schools. The kind of education demanded for their administrators by ecclesiastical and secular governments, or by young merchants in the cities, was not being provided by the monasteries. Both secular governments and the new tightly organized government of the Church by the papacy had developed other means of establishing and keeping public order and no longer relied upon the monasteries for that purpose.

Before 1100 a number of monastic reform movements had begun which encouraged not only moral reform and purification but also an altogether new approach to monasticism, aimed not toward public utility and order, but toward prophecy. The new monk was to withdraw from the world and to practice asceticism and mysticism in order to achieve a deeper religious experience. The new monk was not to be a pillar of societal values, yet he was to have a commitment to society greater than before. His duty was to stand outside the normal values of the Church and of society and to preach their utter transformation, as had the prophets of Israel and Christ himself. For the new monk, attempts to reform society through moderate, progressive measures were futile: what was needed was a radical revolution that would prepare the hearts of men for the Kingdom of God which is not of this world.

The success of these new monastic movements in attracting large numbers of enthusiastic converts to their way of life and even of enlisting the support of kings, nobles, and ordinary people who chose to remain in the world, was amazing. Like that of the monasticism of the third and fourth centuries, this success is partly explicable as a reaction against the advance of ecclesiastical order.

Presages of the new monastic spirit were visible by the mid-eleventh century in men like Peter Damian, who had no use for either imperial or papal order. But toward the end of the century, the new spirit became at once both more radical and more popular. The old Benedictine order could not contain it; and for the first time since the ninth century, new orders were founded, though all were deeply influenced by the Rule of St. Benedict. In broad terms, there were two varieties of the new monasticism, one devoted primarily to ascetic withdrawal and contemplation, the other dedicated to preaching the spirit of prophecy to the world. The two most important orders were the Carthusian and the Cistercian. The Carthusians, founded in 1084 by St. Bruno of Cologne, practiced an almost eremitical life of silence and self-abnegation. Of all orders they kept themselves the most free of corruption, but the very rigors that made this purity possible limited their popularity.

It was the Cistercian order that had the widest influence. About 1075, Robert, a Benedictine abbot, organized a strict community at Molesme. But in 1097 or 1098, Molesme itself seemed to Robert to be growing lax, so he moved to Citeaux to found a new monastery. With the help of Robert of Molesme and Stephen Harding, Robert there restored the Rule of St. Benedict in all its original rigor. Later, in 1119, Stephen Harding wrote the "Charter of Love," which was accepted as the new rule of the order, now called the Cistercian. Rejecting pomp and luxury, the Cistercians banned private property altogether, ate only black bread and water with a few stewed vegetables, emphasized manual labor in place of study and scholarship, slept on rude beds with no other covering than their day clothes in dormitories unheated even in the dead of winter, and refrained from all unnecessary speech. That such a severe life could prove attractive to thousands of people, including men of substance, in a period of general prosperity, is a tribute to the power of the prophetic spirit.

For after an initial period of difficulties the Cistercians began to enjoy a phenomenal success, a success for which St. Bernard of Clairvaux (1091–1153) was more responsible than any other man. The little community at Cîteaux had almost wasted away owing to desertions and disease when, in the winter of 1112, St. Bernard arrived with thirty other novices. Although Bernard had been born into a wealthy family at Fontaines in Burgundy and would have inherited considerable estates, his conscience informed him that Christ had counseled the young rich man to go and sell all that he had and follow him; and at the age of twenty-two Bernard sought out Cîteaux as the strictest monastery he could find. In 1115 he left Cîteaux to found another house obedient to the Cistercian practice in the Vale of Wormwood, a desolate spot which he renamed Clairvaux. By the time of his death he had founded sixty-five Cistercian monasteries and attracted multitudes to join the order.

The vigor and charisma of this man were such that it was said that mothers shut up their sons and wives their husbands when he passed by, for fear that he would lure them away to the monastery. His asceticism was so severe that he declared that mirth was a step on the road to hell, and he was never seen to laugh or to make a joke himself. He practiced mortifications of the flesh beyond those which he enjoined upon others; and when they complained of their hardships, he suggested the whip as remedy. He had no hesitation in reprimanding the great and powerful for their follies. He wrote letters of admonition to the holy Abbot

Suger of Saint-Denis, one of the chief counselors of the kings of France, telling him that his way of life was a disgrace. He led the prosecution of Abelard as a heretic, and he used his personal charisma in the papal schism of 1130–1138 to persuade the kings to accept the candidate he considered the more moral, Innocent II. Bernard's energy was not the product of mental disturbance, harshness, or unkindness. Rather, he was possessed by a love of God so great and consuming that it did not permit him to allow rest either to himself or to others. He gained, and used, his wide political and spiritual influence not for personal aggrandizement, but to preach as a prophet the transformation of the world.

The second group of new orders was that whose first purpose was preaching and for which the ascetic and monastic life was a way to reach the growing numbers of people, particularly in the towns, whom social change and dislocation had to some extent alienated from the faith of their fathers. This task had first been undertaken by the "regular canons." The clergy of the cathedral chapter, who lived together with the bishop, were known as canons. As early as the eighth century, disciplinary efforts had been made to place these canons under a rule. There were also canons living in the so-called collegiate churches, i.e., parish churches in which a number of priests dwelt together. By the beginning of the twelfth century, it was evident that earlier efforts to establish discipline among the canons had not been wholly successful, and this fact, in addition to the recognition of the need for more effective preaching, prompted the foundation of a number of orders of regular canons—secular priests whose commitment was to the world rather than to the cloister, but who adopted a monastic rule for the purposes of strict discipline and whose vigorous preaching was in the prophetic spirit.

There were several of these orders, the Victorines, the Augustinians, and the Premonstratensians, who were the most influential. The Premonstratensians were founded by St. Norbert, a canon of the cathedral chapter of Xanten in the Netherlands, who until the age of about thirty-five lived an easy, even luxurious, life. In 1115 he was caught up by the prophetic spirit and withdrew into a hermitage for three years. Then, recognizing his obligation to teach the transformation of the heart to the world, he began to wander up and down the Rhine preaching. Norbert was at first condemned for preaching without permission, but Pope Calixtus II recognized the utility of such enthusiasm and permitted him to found an order of regular canons with headquarters at Prémontré, a deserted field near Laon in northern France. Like the fully monastic orders, the Premonstratensians practiced fasting and silence as well as other monastic virtues, but they placed a special emphasis upon learning and teaching, so as to prepare themselves to bring the Gospel to the people. Eventually more than two hundred Premonstratensian houses were founded.

By the end of the twelfth century, the Premonstratensian and other canons settled down to a more sedate life, exchanging itinerant preaching for the training of younger preachers in seminaries. The Cistercians had become corrupt, and Cistercians sent to southern France to preach against the Albigensian heretics only encouraged converts to the heresy by means of their bad conduct. A new revival was necessary.

This occurred toward the end of the twelfth century. A young Spanish priest named Dominic, who had come to southern France with his bishop in order to join in the moral struggle against the Albigensians, decided to devote his life to the improvement of both the morality and the intellectual quality of preachers. In 1215, with the approval of Pope Innocent III, he founded the Order of Preachers (Dominicans). The Dominicans and their contemporaries the Franciscans were known as friars (*frères,* "brothers"); both orders of friars continued the work of the regular canons in preaching and teaching to the world. Known as mendicants, because they vowed absolute poverty and lived at first by begging, the friars wandered about Europe preaching wherever the needs of the community demanded. Then with their emphasis upon learning and teaching, the Dominicans gained great influence in the universities. Rational scholasticism was dominated by great Dominican teachers like Albertus Magnus (1206–1280), the teacher of Thomas Aquinas, and Aquinas himself (1226–1274). The Dominicans' devotion to doctrinal truth also led them to participate in less wholesome activities like the Inquisition.

The other chief mendicant order of friars was that founded by St. Francis of Assisi (1181–1226), the Order of Little Brothers (Franciscans), approved by Pope Honorius III in 1223. Francis was the son of Pietro Bernardone, a wealthy cloth merchant in the northern Italian hill town of Assisi. Destined by his father to raise the family status by becoming a knight, Francis took part in one military campaign during which he was captured and held in prison. It was perhaps while he lay sick of fever in prison, meditating upon the meaning of his life, that he determined to turn from the world and to go out and preach the Gospel. This decision was confirmed soon afterwards, when, meeting a leper in the road, he felt compelled by the love of Christ to dismount and to embrace him. The particular virtue of St. Francis is that his love of God after his conversion drew upon the strength of his earlier powerful and joyful love of the world. As a young man he had written beautiful lyric poetry in praise of women; after his conversion his poetry was equally intense in praise of God and God's creatures:

> Praised be my Lord God with all His creatures, and especially our brother the sun, who brings us the day and who brings us the light; fair is he and shines with very great splendor; O Lord, he signifies to us Thee.[3]

His conception of the world was wholly sacred: he recognized the personality of God in his fellow men, in animals, in inanimate objects or even in impersonal forces. He spoke to the birds; he walked out of his way to avoid treading on a worm; and in the agonies of his deathbed he addressed the cauterizing iron as "Brother Fire" and the last bright angel as "Brother Death." Francis was the perfect manifestation of the prophetic spirit, who loved the world with a burning intensity and devotion that com-

---

[3]"The Song of the Creatures," translated by Matthew Arnold.

pelled him to go out and bring it to a recognition of its true nature. In this world that he loved, Francis saw beneath the external appearances to the reality of God's spirit within, and his life was a manifestation of that inner light to others. St. Francis was one of the simplest, and one of the most completely devoted, of Christian mystics.

After leaving his father, who renounced him as an ungrateful madman, Francis withdrew into solitude as a hermit and lived by begging his bread. Having given up his rich clothes, he donned the rough garb and rope belt of a scarecrow, the origin of the brown Franciscan habit. He began to preach to the people and soon attracted disciples from every class of men. At last he founded an order dedicated to preaching, to teaching, and particularly to holy poverty: "I strictly command all the brothers," he said, "never to receive coin or money either directly or through an intermediary."[4] Like the Dominicans, their concern for the teaching of the faith led the Franciscans into education and into the universities, where they pursued experimental science and mysticism—subjects derived from experience—more frequently than logic and metaphysics, the more usual domain of the Dominicans. It is a sad commentary on human nature that almost immediately after the death of its founder, the majority of the Franciscan order abandoned strict poverty and shortly proceeded to brand the more loyal minority, later called the Fraticelli, as heretics.

Popular heresy, like popular devotion, monasticism, and mysticism, was a product of both the reform movement in general and of revulsion against ecclesiastical order in particular. Medieval heresy in the West was always primarily moral rather than theological and popular rather than sacerdotal. From the eighth century, numerous religious dissenters had appeared, most of them Re-

[4]Henry Bettenson, ed. and trans., *Documents of the Christian Church,* 2d ed. (London, 1963), p. 181.

formists, whose zeal for the reform of the Church carried them beyond the limits of orthodox restraint. Such representatives of the prophetic spirit were often admirable for their refusal to compromise the religious spirit in the name of order; often, however, rebellion led them into eccentric, sometimes insane, doctrines. It must be remembered that the pogroms against the Jews and the slaughter of heretics and infidels by the crusading mobs sprang from the same source of unbridled and undisciplined popular zeal.

The tradition of dissent, with its emphasis upon Reformism, remained unchanged until about the mid-twelfth century, but by the eleventh century it had begun to attract both more adherents and more adverse attention from the authorities. Prophetic Reformism continued to be the chief expression of religious dissatisfaction, and between orthodox and heretical prophecy was a thin and often arbitrary line drawn by the authorities. For example, Valdes, a merchant of Lyon, began in the 1170's to wander about the countryside with his followers preaching poverty and a return to apostolic simplicity in terms very similar to those used only a few years later by St. Francis and St. Dominic. But unlike the two saints, Valdes encountered the strong opposition of his bishop, and when he went to Rome to appeal his case, he had the misfortune to be out-talked and humiliated before a papal synod by a smooth, fast-talking, and unsympathetic English prelate. He returned with the laughter of the council ringing in his ears, continued to preach in defiance of the bishop, drifted into more and more extreme condemnations of ecclesiastical order, and was finally branded as a heretic. Between Valdes with his "poor men of Lyon" and Francis with his "little brothers" devoted to poverty, there was little distinction beyond that in their reception, yet one was considered a heretic and the other a saint. On the other hand, the Waldensians, Valdes's followers, remained loyal to his principles in spite of frequent condemnations and persecution, while those of St. Francis, protected and encouraged by the authorities, quickly abandoned his stricter admonitions. Again, religion seems to have benefited less from the approval than from the rejection of society.

In the 1140's a new heresy appeared in western Europe. This was Catharism, a semi-Christian religion of dualism brought to Italy and southern France by Bulgarian missionaries who were members of the Bogomil sect, itself ultimately derived from Middle Eastern Gnosticism. Like the ancient dualist Gnostics, the Catharists believed that there was a cosmic war between the spirit of Good and the spirit of Evil. The spirit of Evil was inferior to that of Good, but it had successfully revolted, and eons would elapse before Good finally triumphed. Good is spirit, and Evil is matter. In its cosmic revolt the spirit of Evil created the universe in order to entrap pure spirits in the prison house of matter. The Old Testament, therefore, is the work of Satan, since it reveres the wicked Creator. Since matter is evil, flesh is evil, and indeed the human body is hideous filth conceived by demons in order to imprison the human spirit. Sexual activity, especially that which might lead to the production of a child, is therefore highly undesirable, for no sin can be worse than to cooperate with the devil in forcing yet another spirit into the flesh. Christ is the messenger sent by the spirit of Good to teach us how to extract our souls from the flesh; being holy, he did not really take on flesh, and, his body being an illusion, he did not really suffer on the Cross. Crucifixes and images, which dignify the body, are therefore inventions of the Devil.

The Catharists absolutely rejected the Christian Church, its priesthood, and its sacraments. Their own sacrament was the "consolation," which was administered to those believers who had shown themselves capable of leading a pure life and which absolved them from all past sin. Those who had received the consolation were called *perfecti*, and they were obliged to abstain from sin entirely, on pain of damnation, since the consolation could not be repeated. For the same reason, some who had received the consolation starved themselves to death afterwards so as to escape the flesh more quickly. Since the consolation was supposed to wipe out all previous sin, many of the simple and less devoted believers put it off till the end of their lives and in the meanwhile allowed themselves carnal pleasures. But the Catharists were sincere enough to make such quantities of converts that by the end of the twelfth century the religion had spread all over northern Europe, particularly in the Low Countries and the Rhineland. In southern France (where they were called Albigensians from their center of Albi) and in northern Italy, they made up such a large portion of the population of all classes that in 1208 Innocent III felt compelled to preach a crusade against them.

The rapid success of the Catharists has a number of causes but only one fundamental explanation: the previous existence of a strong tradition of Reformist dissent. The Reformists, in their ascetic extremism, emphasized the dualist elements latent in the orthodox Christian tradition to the degree that they were ready and willing to accept the stricter dualism of the Catharists. Documents from the Rhineland show the process at work at Cologne: at first there is a report of a Reformist sect; the next report tells of a group within the Reformist sect which is preaching a new and more radical doctrine; and the final document portrays a group completely dominated by Catharism—the whole process having taken only a few years. Catharism, though the most radical heresy which Western Christianity ever faced, owed its success to the demands of the Christian prophetic spirit.

Catharism, as well as much else in southern France, was almost wiped out by the crusade of 1208–1223, after which it gradually dwindled and disappeared. But that hostility to orthodoxy remained at least covertly in southern France can be seen by comparing a map showing the centers of thirteenth-century Catharism with one showing those of sixteenth-century Calvinism: the correspondence is far too striking to be merely coincidental. Meanwhile, the Reformist variety of heresy, which had never been wholly supplanted by Catharism, continued among the Waldensians (more properly: Valdesians) and appeared in new forms throughout the Middle Ages, finally achieving wide success in the Protestant Reformation.

X The Offensive of the Papacy

The growth of the prophetic spirit in the twelfth and thirteenth centuries was matched by the advance of order in Christian society under the leadership of the papacy. From the end of the eleventh century the popes continued to implement their policies by means of crusades, councils, canon law, and the Inquisition. The spirit of reform was perhaps never higher among all sections of the population than it was in the late eleventh and early twelfth centuries; but the two kinds of reform, order and prophecy, were often at variance. These differences of opinion within the Church were brought into relief by the increasing complexity of society: the growth of royal power and of the scope of royal government raised new political difficulties for religion; and the rise of the cities and of the new urban classes made it more difficult to reach the Christian people with an ecclesiastical organization and attitudes designed for a feudal and agricultural society. Finally, the rise of the universities and of scholasticism demanded a complete intellectual reevaluation of the doctrines of the Church.

One of the developments of scholastic thought did much to enhance the theoretical position of the papacy. This was the growth of the structure of canon law. Canon law is the law of the Church stated in the decrees of popes and councils from the earliest Church to the present. It is distinguished from civil law, which derived either from Roman law (as in most of southern Europe) or from customary Germanic law (as in much of northern Europe, especially England). Church courts were usually separate from civil courts and had jurisdiction *in persona*—over clergy and students[1]— and *in re*—over offenses deemed spiritual in nature, like blasphemy or divorce. Until the beginning of the twelfth century, this law had been systematically codified. Then, in imitation of the civil lawyers, who were beginning at that time to restudy and reclassify Roman law according to rational organizational principles, canon lawyers drew up comprehensive codes of canon law. The most important of these canonists of the early twelfth century were Yvo of Chartres, who helped work out the compromises on investitures, and Gratian, who in 1140 published his *Decretum,* or "Concord of Discordant Canons." Gratian not only collected vast numbers of legal texts and organized them systematically but, observing that the laws were often contradictory, undertook to resolve the contradictions by reason. This led to debate, discussion, and reflection upon the nature of the law, which in turn aided the development of political theory.

The free-swinging arguments of the eleventh-century "battle of the books" now yielded to more complex and carefully-worked-out structures of thought. These were at first developed mainly by papalists and so were turned to the support of papal theory. Later they were used by conciliarists concerned with limiting that theory. Many of the greatest popes of the twelfth and thirteenth centuries, like Alexander III (1159–1181), Innocent III (1198–1216), Gregory IX (1227–1241), and Innocent IV (1243–1254) were trained in canon law and used it effectively to advance their position. For example, they elaborated the theory of "plenitude of power," according to which the pope as vicar of Christ has full

[1]Students were considered clergy. The right of clerics to be tried for all crimes in Church courts, where punishments were lighter than in civil courts, was known as "benefit of clergy."

power over all worldly affairs and, therefore, the right to rule temporal as well as spiritual affairs directly. The extensive interference of Innocent III and other popes in secular matters was a reflection of this theory derived from canon law.

The practical implementation of papal policies was an extension of the Gregorian program. Urban II and his successors revived the institution of the permanent legates, they increased wherever they could the number of episcopal sees subject to papal appointment, and they encouraged monastic immunities from the bishops and kings so that the monasteries might be more directly under papal influence.

Urban II undertook a number of policies that materially advanced the papal position. According to the strict dictates of canon law, those bishops consecrated by imperially appointed antipopes did not have proper authority, and therefore ordinations of priests and the sacraments bestowed by those priests were invalid. If the letter of the law had been enforced, there would have been an enormous number of people throughout Europe with invalid orders, invalid baptisms, and invalid marriages. Urban mercifully decided to "dispense from" the canons and to declare these orders and sacraments valid. The dispensation from the canons when generally established was another weapon of papal power, for it permitted the pope to set precedents that would modify or even change tradition.

Urban demonstrated the jurisdiction of papal power throughout society when at the Council of Clermont (1095) he reaffirmed the Truce of God (originated at the beginning of the eleventh century), which outlawed war during certain seasons of the year and on certain days of the week. In the twelfth century the popes also promoted the Peace of God, which protected clergy and other noncombatants at all times. The potentiality for good of a Christian order in society is nowhere clearer than is this systematic attempt to limit war. But then as now, these efforts were unavailing against the arguments of politicians and military men that "realism" demands the pursuit of their policies at whatever cost of ruin and agony. Political "realism" is usually the justification of actions unrealistic by any definitions of humanity or sanity broader than the narrow assumptions of those who argue them.

Under Urban II the papacy for the first time felt secure enough to call an ecumenical council under its presidency. In 1095, Urban held two large councils for the purpose of securing reform and of building papal prestige within the Church and against the temporal powers. One of these was at Piacenza in Italy and the other at Clermont in southern France. Both councils were devoted to attacks upon simony, clerical concubinage, and other vices within the Church and against lay interference in ecclesiastical affairs. Though they themselves did not bear the title ecumenical, they set the stage for the ecumenical councils of the Middle Ages, of which there were six: I Lateran (1123), II Lateran (1139), III Lateran (1179), IV Lateran (1215), I Lyon (1245), and II Lyon (1274). These medieval councils were characterized by papal domination. They were all summoned by the popes and used to advance the order and reform of the Church under papal leadership. The decline of papal power after 1300 is visible in the fact that the first ecumenical council called after that date (Vienne, 1311), was dominated by King Philip IV of France, evidence that both empire and papacy were yielding to the new nationalism.

At the Council of Clermont in 1095, Urban launched the First Crusade, a holy war to liberate the holy places from the Moslems. The surprising spectacle of the vicar of the Prince of Peace preaching conquest and blood can be understood only in the context of the growing rigidity and exclusiveness of medieval Christianity, which was turned not only against Islam but against heresy, Judaism, and Eastern Orthodoxy as well.

Until the eleventh century, heretics had been treated with mildness and restraint, suffering no more than reprimands or harassment. Now murders of heretics by mobs like the one that killed

Ramihrd in 1077 became common, and executions by kings and other secular princes began when in 1022 King Robert the Pious of France burned some heretics at Orléans. In the eleventh and twelfth centuries, the secular authorities increased their vigor in detecting the heretics and their severity in punishing them. Frederick II of Germany and Sicily, for example, made death by burning a mandatory sentence for heresy in 1231. The Church, in recognition of Christian mercy, never executed anyone for heresy: it conducted the investigations, arraigned and tried the dissenters, and, if they were found guilty, turned them over to the secular arm for "proper attention" *(animadversione debita),* which meant hanging or the stake.

In 1184 the prosecution of heretics was formalized by the Council of Verona under Lucius III, who ordered every bishop to conduct an inquisition in his own diocese. In its origins, the inquisition was neither horrible nor unusual: it was a variation of the "inquests" made by medieval monarchs or their representatives. These inquests or investigations might consist of surveys for the purpose of taxation, like Domesday Book, or investigations by a grand jury for crimes in their area of jurisdiction. In another respect, the episcopal inquisition was an extension of the bishop's powers of visitation, under which he had the duty to tour the parishes of his diocese making sure that proper discipline was kept. By the decree of Verona he was now simply expected to pay particular attention to the maintenance of doctrinal orthodoxy.

In 1231 a papal inquisition was established at Rome by Pope Gregory IX, with powers to investigate heresy throughout the Church. In 1233 he made the Dominican order particularly responsible for the extirpation of heresy. The papal inquisition later became a permanent institution, named the Holy Office, for the repression of dissent. The papal inquisition was nothing like as vicious as the later Spanish inquisition, and the horrors even of that body have been exaggerated by novelists and propagandists. But the practices of the papal inquisition were distasteful enough. In accordance with principles of Roman law and of traditional Germanic law, the defendant was held to be guilty unless he could prove himself innocent—which was difficult because the identity of his accusers and sometimes even the specific charges were withheld from the accused in order to protect informers from revenge. Heresy was deemed such a terrible offense that no one could be convicted unless he confessed, and so efforts to secure confessions became steadily more zealous, the use of torture being formally permitted by the canon lawyer Pope Innocent IV in his bull *Ad extirpanda* (1252). When the confession was elicited, the victim was handed over to the secular arm for due attention. Sometimes, of course, the accused was acquitted; or if the offense was his first and he repented, he was allowed to go after being given a certain penance, sometimes a whipping or the wearing in public of distinctive clothing.

The inquisitors have been considered sadists or thieves, depending upon whether one's attention is beguiled more by the spectacle of torture or by the confiscation of the heretics' property. Both accusations, while doubtless justly levied at a few individuals, are unhelpful as generalizations. The inquisitors considered heresy a pernicious disease affecting the soul and therefore a worse danger than any physical plague. No mercy could be shown the heretics' bodies lest they corrupt the immortal souls of others. It was with complete sincerity, and often with great reluctance, that the inquisitors followed their profession. When the logic of the spirit of order and authority within the Church went unchecked by mercy or common sense, it permitted Christians to torture and kill other Christians with good will and a sense of piety. The attitude of the papal legate Arnold Amalric at the siege of Carcassonne, during the Albigensian crusade, is illustrative. He ordered the entire city to be put to the torch. When an attendant suggested that there were orthodox Christians as well as heretics within its walls, he replied, "Go ahead and burn it, for God will know his own." The innocent would go to their heavenly reward, and as for the guilty, flames were their proper environment.

Why should the attitude of the Church, so patient with heretics for centuries, have changed in the eleventh century, when the spirit of reform was at its height? Partly because the heretics were somewhat more numerous and more radical than before. Partly because heretical sects were better organized and because, from the twelfth century, they were tied in with movements of social and economic unrest and were therefore more socially dangerous. But most importantly, precisely *because* the reform spirit was at its height. The same widespread and fervent breath of reform that made people long to go on pilgrimages, to enter ascetic monasteries, and to become mystics also impelled them to attack and murder heretics and Jews and to undertake holy wars against the Moslems. Religious zeal is a powerful force for love and humanity and purity. When it is willing to sacrifice even one human being to theory and ideology, it can be an equally powerful force for inhumanity. This inhumanity was encouraged by the growing rigidity and exclusiveness of the Church. Identifying the Mystical Body of Christ with membership in the visible Church, canon lawyers defined the Church as those who were in communion with the bishop of Rome. Those who were disobedient to Rome were cut off from the Body of Christ; they were limbs of Satan, damned, and unworthy of consideration as human beings. This tendency to regard one's enemies as less than human is one with which we are not unfamiliar in the twentieth century.

The same arguments that were applied to heretics were also applied to Jews, and the same transition from tolerance to persecution occurred in the course of the reform movement of the eleventh and twelfth centuries. In the diaspora, especially following the sack of Jerusalem in 70 A.D., the Jews had fled Palestine to settle in the cities of the Mediterranean and western Europe, particularly in Spain, where they were called Sephardic Jews and where they built an illustrious culture. In most of the cities in which they settled, they chose to live together in ghettos in order to preserve their identity in the midst of a population at first pagan and then Christian. The Jewish community was tightly organized around the synagogue under the leadership of the rabbi, and it had its own schools, where Hebrew was taught, its own laws and law courts, and its own taxes and tax collection.

This state of affairs was by and large perfectly tolerated by the Christians. Religious arguments were often heated in a period when both Christians and Jews took their religion more seriously than they do now, but these arguments generally remained on a theoretical level, and there were Christian converts to Judaism as well as Jewish converts to Christianity. Christian scholars valued the Hebrew scholarship of the rabbis, and a Christian king like Louis the Pious valued their literacy and employed many Jews in his administration. On the rare occasions when there were popular outbreaks against the Jews, as in Palermo at the end of the sixth century when the synagogue was plundered and burned, the authorities intervened and enforced strict restitution to the injured. The discrimination of the Visigothic law code against Jews was unusual and should be seen in the context of the more frequent discriminations in law of Arian against Catholic or Catholic against Arian, Christians all. As late as the twelfth century, the Christian citizens of Sens could view with equanimity the erection of a synagogue steeple higher than that of the cathedral.

But already under Louis the Pious the first signs of future distress were visible. Evidently irked by royal patronage of the Jews, Archbishop Agobard of Lyon wrote the first violent anti-Jewish tract of the Middle Ages. Then, from the ninth century onwards, increasing order in society as a whole worked to the general disadvantage of the Jews. The feudal relationship, which demanded the use of a Christian oath in the ceremony of investiture, drove Jews off the land into the growing cities, where they engaged in commerce and in the crafts. But in the eleventh and twelfth centuries the rise of artisans' gilds, each organized around the cult of a particular saint, drove the Jews out of the crafts. They were left with banking, moneychanging, and moneylending, activities condemned as unfit for (though often clandestinely pursued by) Christians.

Now to basic religious antagonism and to the Christian irritation at the Jews' deliberate isolation of themselves from the Christian community was added a fatal motive of economic envy. Little pity was shown to the many Jews who grew poor because they were excluded from the crafts, but much envy was directed against the few who grew wealthy at banking and lending. In an age when all commercial ventures were adventures in the original sense of the word, moneylending was particularly risky, and as a consequence interest rates had to be high. The effect, not the cause, attracted the reproach and bitterness of the Christians.

Then in the eleventh century came a wave of popular religious zeal combined with a legalism that excluded Jews more strictly than before from any participation in the general community. The same urge that sent tens of thousands of peasants from western Europe to Constantinople to crusade against the Moslems impelled them to stop along the way to kill infidels closer to home. In one city after another, particularly along the Rhine, the crusaders stopped and looted and burned the Jewish ghettos, putting to death those who would not accept baptism. The pogrom was now invented; it was to continue, first in western and then in eastern Europe, down to the final holocaust under the Nazis. Popular beliefs concerning the Jews grew wilder, and in obedience to an unpleasant psychological regularity, they took forms similar to the Romans' beliefs about the Christians or, later, certain Protestants' beliefs about the Catholics. The Jews kidnapped Christian children and killed them in a ritual murder that was an inherent part of the Jewish religion. The Jews poisoned wells. The Jews practiced cannibalism and magic. Most absurdly of all, the Jews, who were hated for their denial of the Christian sacraments, were accused of stealing the blessed sacrament from churches and profaning it. Their favorite game, apparently, was to take the Host and stab it with a knife; occasionally the villains would be found out by a just miracle, for the wounded Host would bleed unquenchably until the blood, flowing out of the door, attracted the attention of the righteous Christian people.

The attitude of the authorities toward these absurd beliefs and the outrageous persecutions they provoked was at first adequately severe. The bishops of the Rhenish cities whose Jews were attacked by the mobs took great pains, sometimes at the risk of their own lives, to hide or otherwise protect them. St. Bernard declared the persecutors of the Jews heretics, and Pope Gregory X officially refuted the charges of ritual murder as nonsense. But gradually the official position hardened, particularly in regard to converted Jews who relapsed into Judaism, and Innocent III went so far as to demand that the Jews wear distinctive clothing. For the most part, the ecclesiastical authorities refrained from official persecutions, but more frequently than not they remained silent in the face of popular outrages or the repressive policies of the Christian kings.

It was the Christian princes who were the most persistent, if not the bloodiest, in their persecutions, and here the motive was plainly money. The Lombards and the Templars, both of whom had amassed wealth by banking and lending, were treated with as much violence as the Jews, though the Jews were often subjected to peculiar humiliations. An English law of 1222 ordered every Jew above the age of six to wear a distinctive yellow badge upon his clothing, an ultimate antecedent of the yellow star of David imposed by the Nazis. Philip IV of France (1285–1314), Edward I of England (1272–1307), Ferdinand and Isabella of Spain (1479 –1504), and other rulers used religious arguments as an excuse to confiscate the property of the Jews and expel them from their domains.

The hostility of Western Christendom to the heretics and the Jews extended to the Moslems and, to a lesser degree, the Byzantine Christians. This hostility took the form of the crusade or holy war. The idea of holy war was an old one, the Byzantine Emperor Heraclius having preached it when the Moslems first conquered the Holy Land in 637. Charlemagne crusaded against the Moslems in Spain and extended the concept of holy war to the pagans when he converted the Saxons by force. The idea of the crusades was to rescue Christian people and to regain Christian territories (or to add to them) from the unbelievers. The symbol of the crusaders' purpose came to be the holy places, particularly the Holy Sepulchre (the church built over what is supposed to be the tomb of Christ) in Jerusalem.

The era of concentrated Crusades began in 1095 when Urban II preached the First Crusade at Clermont. The conventional numbering of the Crusades is not particularly helpful, for they were not clearly separated or defined. What is significant is that from 1095 there were frequent expeditions of Western Christians (called Franks by the Easterners) to the East. Some of these expeditions were led by kings and some by noblemen and knights; some were mere mobs of peasants; some were equipped by Italian cities as ventures for profit; one consisted entirely of children; and one was wholly peaceful—that of Frederick II of Germany in 1227–1229. That emperor, whose devotion to Christianity was not notable, spent his time in the Holy Land exchanging entertainment, theological debate, and commercial concessions with his Moslem hosts. From 1099 until 1291, the Franks maintained states on the eastern shore of the Mediterranean, but even after these were destroyed, the struggle continued. The war against the Moslems continued in Spain, from which the Moors were finally completely expelled in 1492; in the islands and along the coasts of the eastern Mediterranean and North Africa; and eventually in the Balkans against the Ottoman Turks. The holy war was also extended against other enemies: the pagans of the eastern Baltic, whom the Teutonic Knights (a Germanic military-religious order) conquered, and the Albigensian heretics of southern France, subdued in a bloody war lasting from 1208 to 1213.

Many causes of the Crusades have been adduced. They were a manifestation of the age-old struggle between East and West. They were part of a long tradition of Christian holy war, or a righteous effort to regain territories seized from Christendom by force. They were a cynical effort to obtain land and wealth. They were part of the commercial expansion of western Europe, or mass movements symptomatic of social unrest and discontent at home. They were a program to enhance the prestige of the papacy. They were the product of superstitious fanaticism. All of these interpretations are partly true, but an examination of the religious and social environment of the precise time in which they were generated yields explanations similar to those for the persecution of heretics and Jews. The Crusades, whatever else they were, were an expression of the reforming zeal of the period, taking the form of popular fanaticism on the one hand, and of papal legalism and exclusivism on the other.

The results of the Crusades are impressive mainly for their destructiveness. To begin with, there was the enormous expenditure of blood and suffering on all sides. Of the peasant mobs that set out for the Holy Land in 1096, none ever reached their destination: either they despaired and went home; or they were murdered by robbers and bandits; or they died of disease or malnutrition; or if they got as far as Asia Minor, they were massacred by the Turks. Many of the children who set out in 1212 for the Holy Land were killed or sold into slavery. The pogroms in Europe, slaughter of Moslems and Jews in the sack of Jerusalem by the Franks in 1099, and the rape of Constantinople by its Frankish allies in 1204 are only a few illustrations of the savagery meted out by the Christians to their enemies.

In exchange for all this horror, nothing of permanent value was obtained. The Crusader states in the East lasted awhile and then were wiped out, leaving Jerusalem permanently in the hands of the Moslems. The Moslems, heretofore relatively tolerant of the Christians in their domains, now returned violence for violence, and their counter-crusades eventually brought their banners to the walls of Vienna. The schism between the Eastern and the Western Churches was made unbridgeable by the notorious Fourth Crusaders of 1202–1204. Sent by Innocent III to relieve the Christian forces in the Holy Land, they took passage with greedy Venetian shipowners, who persuaded them to champion the cause of a pretender to the Byzantine throne. After they had begun by sacking the Christian port of Zara, the pope tried to call them back, but it was too late. They proceeded to Constantinople, where they imposed their candidate for the throne by force, and then, when he proved unable to pay the tribute they insisted upon in return, they put the city to the sword. The soldiers of Christ looted churches, fired the city, and raped and killed at will. As a result, the Byzantine Empire was temporarily dismantled and permanently debilitated, making its eventual conquest by the Turks in 1453 almost inevitable. The natural distrust of Byzantine leaders for the West was so great that when in 1439 the Emperor John VIII agreed to accept papal supremacy in order to secure Western aid against the Turks, they refused to approve, saying that they would rather see the Sultan's turban than a cardinal's hat in Constantinople. Even today, the memory of 1204 has made it more difficult to secure ecumenical cooperation between the Eastern and Western Churches.

One outcome of the Crusades is immensely significant in Christian history because it did not happen: the conversion of the Mongols. Oddly, this was well within the realm of possibility in the thirteenth century. The Mongols and the other tribes of central Asia had been evangelized by Nestorian Christians, and at the time of the Crusades there were several Christian generals, nobles, and even princesses among the Mongol leaders and their people. The Franciscan missionary William of Rubruck found in his journey to the East in 1253–1254 that there were numerous Nestorian churches and practicing Christians throughout central Asia, even in Karakorum, the Mongol capital, and that there was a bishop of the Nestorians at Peking.

The Mongol Empire had not adopted any higher religion and was consequently subject to the influence of them all. It was possible that a vigorous missionary effort could have established the religion of Christ from the Atlantic to the Pacific. The political situation in the late thirteenth century was particularly conducive to such success, for the Mongols were engaged in the conquest of Moslem Persia and Mesopotamia, and they considered the possibility of an alliance with the Christians against their common enemy. Missions were sent by Kublai Khan to the courts of Louis IX in France and of Edward I of England, and a Mongol representative was at the Council of II Lyon in 1274. In 1286 Argun, the Khan of Persia, dispatched an embassy under a Nestorian monk, a close friend of the Nestorian patriarch, to the court of Pope Honorius IV, from which he went on to see Edward I and Philip IV. In 1291, Argun sent a letter to the West proposing a joint attack upon the Moslems in Syria and promising that the Mongols would turn over Jerusalem to the Crusaders.

But to all these opportunities the Christians prove incapable of responding. The kings were occupied with national struggles in the West; the people were tired of the Crusades; and in 1291 the last stronghold in the Crusader states, the fortress of Acre, fell to the Moslems. No Christian forces came to join the Mongol armies in the war, and though the Franciscan missionaries exerted themselves for years in the East under great hardships and with some success, the Mongols as a whole lost interest in Christianity. Christian missions continued to exist in China until the decline of Mongol power in the fourteenth century, when the Chinese nationalists drove out or executed the Christians as another manifestation of the foreign influence they detested. It was not that the energy of the missionaries failed, but that Western Christendom proved unable to marshal the energies and resources requisite to the conversion of the East. Effective penetration of the East was left to the merchants, the Polos of the thirteenth century and their successors in the fourteenth, fifteenth, and sixteenth— when the great age of European expansion was undertaken not by the followers of heaven, but by those of this world. Those who sought the triumph of a Christian order had, almost without realizing it, lost one of their greatest opportunities.

The struggle of the papacy with the temporal powers had not come to an end with the accession of Lothar II in 1125. From that moment the preeminence of papacy over empire was assured, but there were many battles yet to wage, not only with the emperor but also with the kings of England and France.

The example of England illustrates the perennial nature of the conflict. In England, royal power over the Church had always been extensive, though it had likewise always been exerted in the cause of reform. William the Conqueror had obtained the throne with the blessing of Pope Alexander II, and the new king made it clear that he was going to exercise as full control over spiritual as he did over temporal affairs. As archbishop of Canterbury he appointed the reform abbot of Bec, Lanfranc (1070–1089), and with him carried out a reorganization and purification of the English Church. Honor was rendered the pope as the head of Christendom, Peter's pence continued to be paid, and the Church in England continued to profess itself a most loyal daughter of Rome. But in practical matters, the king, aided by his archbishop, ruled supreme. He continued to appoint bishops, he reorganized the dioceses, he separated the Church from the civil courts, and he declared that his permission was necessary in order to receive a papal letter, to recognize a pope, or to excommunicate any of the king's barons or ministers.

As long as a just king ruled the Church, the pope was obliged to consider the situation tolerable, and in 1081 Gregory VII wrote a letter to William indicating that the latter's virtues required that his vices be treated with patience. But the death of the Conqueror in 1087 was followed by that of Lanfranc in 1089, and the potentiality for conflict was now realized. William's successor, William II, inherited his father's will to control the Church without his interest in reforming it. From 1089 to 1093 William left the see of Canterbury vacant in order to collect its revenues. At last the king was persuaded to accept Anselm, Lanfranc's successor as abbot of Bec, as his successor in the see of Canterbury (1093–1109). But meanwhile, Anselm had been swayed by the radicalism of the papal revolution, and he arrived in England determined to limit the king's power. He demanded the return of the Church properties confiscated by the king after the death of Lanfranc, and he defended the monks from the inroads made on their properties by royalist bishops. Anselm was able to win the support of many of the bishops to the cause of reform and to secure, as well, the support of some of the nobility, who welcomed an opportunity to embarrass the king.

There now began that curious alliance between the Church and the English nobility against the rising power of the king, an alliance that was to be called into being time and time again until the final triumph of the king during the Protestant Reformation. Now, in spite of opposition, William II succeeded in driving Anselm into exile on the Continent, where he remained until William's brother Henry I (1100–1135) ascended the throne. Henry, more of his father's temperament than of his brother's, recalled Anselm from exile. But in the meanwhile, Anselm, like the course of the revolution itself, had become much more radical and now refused to consecrate bishops who had received lay investiture. Anselm was driven out for the third time in 1105. A compromise on investitures was reached in 1107, which left the king in firm control of the Church. When Henry died, however, the succession was disputed between his daughter Matilda and her cousin Stephen, and the Church and the nobility were able to win concessions from both sides.

The struggle was resumed under Matilda's son Henry II (1154–1189). An able and vigorous king, Henry was determined to restore the power and prerogatives of the monarch to what they had been at the time of his grandfather Henry I. As his archbishop of Canterbury, he appointed the son of a Norman merchant family of London, a man who had been his drinking, hunting, and wenching companion for years and who had recently served as an able and industrious chancellor with every sign of complete loyalty to his monarch. This was Thomas Becket of Cheapside, whose personality now underwent a striking change. Impressed either by the spiritual responsibility of his new office or by its political power, he undertook as archbishop to assert the independence of the bishops from the king and the prerogatives of the papacy.

Thomas became archbishop in 1161, and by 1163 he and Henry had already quarreled. The issue that provoked the quarrel, though in itself minor, had broad implications. In order to increase the deterrent to crime and thereby to promote law and order, the king wished to take clergymen who had been found guilty of a civil crime in an ecclesiastical court and try them again in a civil court, where they could be given a stiffer penalty. Thomas's refusal to cooperate enraged his old friend; and in 1164 Henry promulgated the Constitutions of Clarendon, which claimed for the king all the rights, and more, that William the Conqueror had enjoyed over the Church. Most of the bishops yielded to the king, some venally, some in good faith that the old tradition of royal reform could be retained; but Becket refused and fled to the Continent. From exile he wrote Henry in 1166, "It is certain that kings receive their power from the Church, and the Church hers from Christ alone." In the hope of reaching an agreement, Thomas returned to England, but neither king nor archbishop was willing to yield what seemed to him a position that was just and right. On December 29, 1170, four knights, convinced rightly or wrongly that they were doing the will of the king, assaulted the archbishop in his cathedral and murdered him before the high altar.

T. S. Eliot's *Murder in the Cathedral* presents a view of the conflict of prophecy and order in the archbishop's mind as he debates whether or not to face martyrdom. In the play, there are five tempters. The first three promise the archbishop temporal delights or powers if he will cease his opposition to the king. But the fourth tempter encourages him to martyrdom as a way to personal glory, an example of the false spiritual pride that can afflict the prophetic spirit. The fifth tempter (in the form of the women of Canterbury) begs him to yield to the king and thereby avoid hurting them by stirring up trouble. In this appeal, as in the suggestion of the second tempter that king and archbishop should work smoothly together to build the common good, the spirit of order appears, with all the attractions of easy compromise.

Eliot's archbishop triumphs over all temptations and submits resolutely to the will of God; what was in the real Becket's mind we can hardly say. But in any event the consequences of the murder were hardly satisfactory to Henry. Thomas became a popular martyr, and the general disgust for the assassination all over Europe obliged the king to do penance at Avranches in 1172 and to renounce most of the disputed royal claims.

For the next few decades a working compromise obtained, during which papal powers over the English Church slowly increased. The next crisis came under King John (1199–1216) and Archbishop Stephen Langton (1207–1228). Here again the Church and the nobility made common cause against a king who was pursuing a policy that was not only vigorous but unscrupulous and by any standards, feudal or Christian, immoral. In this struggle, which culminated in Magna Carta (1215) and in which Pope Innocent III (1198–1216) and his legates directly intervened, Stephen Langton tried to work out a compromise that would secure the best interests of the king and the pope, while protecting episcopal independence as much as possible from both. But in the course of the struggle the pope intervened to the extent of placing all England under an interdict (1208) and excommunicating (1209) and deposing (1213) the king. Like Henry IV at Canossa, John hastily yielded in order to secure papal support against his enemies at home. He declared himself the pope's vassal and England a papal fief. Throughout the succeeding century, the pope and his legates attempted to enforce their suzerainty over England. In this they had generally little success, but it was true, nonetheless, that during the thirteenth century the papacy had more influence over English ecclesiastical affairs than at any time before or after.

The policies of Innocent III in regard to John illustrate the enormous temporal power that the papacy had learned to wield. The pope, basing his claim to direct temporal policy on the theory of plenitude of power enunciated by the canon lawyers, could use four weapons against a king: interdict (which by prohibiting all distribution of the sacraments, including baptism and matrimony, throughout the entire realm was designed to stir up popular pressure against the king), excommunication, formal deposition, and the ban (which combined excommunication and deposition). In addition, the enormous political powers of the papacy could be brought to bear. Stalin's question "How many divisions does the pope have?" would not have been asked ironically in the thirteenth century. For example, in his attack upon King John, Innocent III called upon Philip II of France for help; and that king, only eager to strike at his old enemy, launched an invasion of the island, which was repulsed after papal approval was withdrawn in reward for John's submission to Rome.

The intervention of Innocent III in imperial politics illustrates papal political power even more clearly. The declining power of the emperors had already contributed to the rise of that of the popes, and now, after the death of the Emperor Henry VI in 1196, occurred a period of disputed succession. The throne was claimed by both Otto of Brunswick and Philip of Swabia, and in the midst of civil war Innocent issued the decretal *Venerabilem*, declaring that he had a right to decide between the two candidates. Eventually both died, and the throne passed to Philip's nephew Frederick II (1212–1250). Frederick, though powerful in Sicily, was never able to control Germany effectively, and after his death there ensued another period of civil war that further weakened imperial authority. Innocent intervened not only in England and Germany but in France, Bulgaria, Norway, Aragon, and many other territories. His temporal authority was further demonstrated by the leadership he exerted in the inception of the Fourth Crusade and the war against the Albigensians.

The exercise of temporal power on the part of Innocent III was not without precedent. It sprang not from any claim to direct temporal rights but from the theory that the pope was charged with the rule of all Christian society as the vicar of Christ, a papalist theory that had been developing from the time of Gelasius I through the reign of Gregory VII and was now culminating. What Innocent had in mind was not a theocracy but a united Christian society, in which the pope had the duty to oblige princes to rule in accordance with the principles of divine justice. Innocent's theories were the strongest expression to that date of the idea that the construction and maintenance of a Christian order depended upon the strength and authority of the pope as the vicar of Christ over all of society. The pope had "not only the universal Church but the whole world to govern.... Peter alone assumed the plenitude of power. You see then," Innocent explained in a letter to the archbishop of Ravenna, "who is this servant set over the household, truly the vicar of Jesus Christ, successor of Peter, anointed of the Lord, a God of Pharaoh, set between God and man, lower than God but higher than man, who judges all and is judged by no one."[1]

These papalist theories were given their strongest expression by Benedetto Gaetani, who ascended the papal throne in 1294 as Pope Boniface VIII. The very election of Boniface was a triumph of the spirit of order over the spirit of prophecy. A few months previously, a hermit named Pietro di Murrone had been dragged from his cell and forced to accept the papacy as Pope Celestine V. Celestine used his short period of power to endorse the struggles of the spiritual Franciscans, against the lax majority of the order, to reinstate the original rule of St. Francis. But he was unable to cope successfully with the machinations of the powerful cardinals who wished to use him as a tool, and resigned the papacy, dying shortly after.

The ardent exponent of papalist order, Boniface VIII, was the successor of the unhappy defender of prophecy. Boniface was a man whose natural tendencies to rashness were encouraged by the extreme difficulties under which he was obliged to labor as pope. He was accused by envious detractors of having managed the resignation and even the death of his predecessor, and he never lived down the reputation for unscrupulousness that these rumors—probably unjustly—gave him. He was threatened in central Italy by a combination of hostile cardinals and certain families of the Roman nobility, of whom the most antagonistic was the Colonna family; in southern Italy the Aragonese had taken Sicily away from the papal allies, the Angevins; and he was under pressure to call a crusade to regain the Holy Land, whose last Christian fortress, Acre, had fallen in 1291. Most important, he was challenged by the rising power of the kings of France and England.

[1]Translated by Brian Tierney, in his *The Crisis of Church and State, 1050–1300* (Englewood Cliffs, N.J., 1964), p. 132.

167

While the empire and the kingdom of Germany had lost most of its power to influence papal policies, France and England were becoming yearly more wealthy, more unified, and more determined to establish and to preserve their natural identities. In France Philip IV (1285–1314) and in England Edward I (1272–1307), engaged in expansive foreign policies and in increasing the size and strength of their governments, were faced with a financial crisis and sought new means of raising tax monies. Both hit upon the solution of imposing a regular and fairly high tax upon the clergy. The clergy had on previous specific occasions been asked for aid, as when the kings were planning crusades, but it had become common to ask for such aid in the name of a crusade even when the king had no intention of ever going on one. Now for the first time a tax of the clergy was imposed for general purposes.

The response of Boniface VIII touched off a struggle that eventually dealt papalism a deadly blow. It was an unjudicious, even violent, response, but it was one in the tradition of Gregory VII and Innocent III, whose ideas Boniface was attempting to carry out in his own extreme fashion. His immediate response to the kings' taxation was the bull *Clericis laicos* (1296), forbidding such policies. But both kings were under too much fiscal pressure to accept such a judgment. In England, the king attempted to seize Church property and was only restrained by the fact that the clergy and nobility made common cause of their grievances against the growing power of the monarchy. In France, the king put an embargo on the export of gold and silver, in effect preventing the clergy from sending taxes to the pope, and in addition pressed policies, like the liability of bishops to trial for treason, aimed at establishing his authority over the pope.

A long series of angry exchanges began, ending in the issuing of the bull *Unam Sanctam* by Boniface in 1302. *Unam Sanctam* is one of the strongest statements of the papalist theory of order ever issued: "Therefore, if the earthly power errs," it stated, "it shall be judged by the spiritual power..., but if the supreme spiritual power errs it can be judged only by God, and not by man.... Therefore we declare, state, define, and pronounce that it is altogether necessary to salvation for every human creature to be subject to the Roman pontiff."[2] Though this was a fulfillment of traditional papalist theory and not the mad ravings of a megalomaniac, as some nineteenth-century historians implied, it was a position that could be successfully countered by the newly powerful kingdoms of the west.

Philip IV replied to *Unam Sanctam* by declaring the pope a usurper and a heretic and threatening to summon a council to depose him and elect a new pope. By August, 1303, Boniface was preparing a bull of excommunication against Philip; and to prevent this, Philip's counselor Guillaume de Nogaret, with the help of Sciarra Colonna, burst into the papal castle of Anagni on September 7, 1303, and seized the pope. Soon afterward Boniface died, and by 1305 Philip had secured not only the election of a pope submissive to him but the removal of the seat of the papacy, for the only time in its history, away from Rome. Arguing that at Rome the popes were too subject to the political influences of the Roman nobility, Philip established the papacy at Avignon in southern France.

For the purpose of securing order in Christian society, the papacy had prosecuted heretics and Jews, preached crusades, and founded the inquisition. In the name of order, too, it had brought down the empire. Now the kings were to bring down the papacy, and with it the ideal of a united Christian society based upon the theological doctrine of the Mystical Body of Christ and the memory of the *imperium romanum.* In the meantime, the search for order was carried on in the realm of the intellect as well as in that of politics.

[2]*Ibid.,* p. 189.

xi The Scholastic Order, 1050–1300

Scholasticism represents the search for order in intellectual life. Scholasticism was, by its most literal definition, the theology and philosophy taught in the great schools of western Europe from the eleventh through fourteenth centuries. And in one sense its cause was the growth of population that promoted the development of the episcopal schools in the cities, where students and teachers from all over Europe drew together. Paris, Oxford, Bologna, Toulouse—these and other great centers of learning, which in the thirteenth century developed into universities, encouraged the exchange of ideas in a stimulating atmosphere. Within this atmosphere, scholasticism was (by a more precise definition) the creation of a new method to deal with and to assimilate the new philosophical and scientific materials that were being introduced.

These new materials were mostly very old: works of Aristotle and other ancient Greek philosophers and scientists that had been lost to the West owing to the general ignorance of Greek. They had always been known, though not generally used, in the Eastern empire, and in the seventh and eighth centuries the Moslem conquerors of the Near East translated them first into Syriac and then into Arabic. They then went on to use them as the basis for a brilliant culture, with its centers at Baghdad and Córdoba. With the aid of these books, the Arabs thrust far ahead of the West in medicine, mathematics, and astronomy; and Moslem philosophers, including Avicenna (980–1037) and Averroës (1126–1178), grappled with the problems of reconciling Greek learning with Moslem revelation. The same problems were posed to the Jewish philosophers of Spain, like ibn-Gabirol (c. 1020–1070) and Moses Maimonides (1135–1204).

The Christians remained in happy ignorance of these problems until the mid-eleventh century, relying upon Plato and the Platonically expressed thought of the Church fathers and Augustine. Some of Aristotle's works were known and respected, but much of his more advanced logic and almost all of his science had been lost. Then, in Sicily, southern Italy, and Spain, where contacts between Islam and Christianity were common, Christian scholars began to make translations of the lost works from the Arabic, the task continuing into the twelfth and thirteenth centuries. Since the original Greek texts had by this time been expanded and elaborated by the commentaries of the Arab philosophers, the result was the importation not only of many unfamiliar Greek ideas, but of Moslem theories based upon Neoplatonic and other exotic doctrines with which early Christianity had come into contact but had never wished to assimilate.

The effect upon twelfth-century Christian philosophers and scientists was radical: suddenly at hand were materials with which their view of the world could be at once rendered more precise and enormously expanded. Theologians—and most of the philosophers of the Middle Ages were theologians—then had to decide whether to condemn the new materials outright or to assimilate them into a new system. Throughout the period, conservatives attempted to eject the new ideas from theology, even attempting to have their study banned at the schools, and it was agreed even by the most progressive that some were indeed irreconcilable with Christianity. But gradually theologians responded to the challenge by creating

171

new systems. The choice was as clear to them as it had been to the Moslem and Jewish theologians: either reconcile the new knowledge with revelation or permit a deep chasm to be formed between faith and reason.

Theologians of the nineteenth and twentieth centuries have been faced with similar problems in the wake of the great changes in modern science, but their response has been by and large less vigorous than that of their medieval predecessors, partly because the sheer quantity of modern knowledge daunts all efforts to synthesize. A twentieth-century theologian who attempted to do with evolution what the scholastics did with Aristotle was Pierre Teilhard de Chardin, whose *Phenomenon of Man* integrates revelation and evolution in a new theological system. Most modern Christian thought, however, accepts both revelation and science without attempting to synthesize them—thus embracing the doctrine of the "two truths" (roundly condemned by theologians of the thirteenth century), which assumes that there is no one truth and that scientific and philosophical truth may differ from revealed truth.

The effort of the scholastics was to work out a synthesis between the old and the new knowledge. The question was how to go about it. After the establishment of schools where ideas could be exchanged, the next requisite was the development of an effective method of assimilation that could be generally accepted by scholars. For almost a millennium, theological, philosophical, and scientific disputes had been referred for solution to the "authorities" of the past: the Bible, the classics, and the Church fathers. Following Plato, Paul, and Augustine, the mode of philosophical expression was allusive, allegorical, repetitive. To the modern mind, it often appears to wander far afield before returning to the point.

Now in the course of the twelfth century, a wholly new mode of expression was developed. This method was logically consequent, beginning, like Aristotle and Euclid, from axioms and proceeding from deduction to higher deduction and to lateral corollaries until from one trunk a thousand ramifications had spread, creating a new and coherent system. Even the derivation of the axioms was in part new. They were still largely drawn from the Bible, the fathers, and

172

the classics; but sometimes, in imitation of Aristotle, they were drawn from sense experience. The first of Aquinas's famous five proofs of the existence of God, for example, begins by postulating from sense experience alone that we observe the existence of motion in the universe. From that postulate he draws deduction after deduction until he arrives at a prime mover whom, he says, all men call God. This building of theological systems not on the basis of revelation, but on the basis of natural philosophy was called natural theology, and it proceeded in the same way as the speculative metaphysics of the ancient Greeks. Then, after drawing all they could from the premises of natural theology, philosophers like Aquinas superimposed revelation upon the structure of natural theology and proceeded to draw from the priniciples of revelation what deductions they could. This part of the process was called revealed theology. When finished, the process formed a coherent system of the world, leaving out nothing relating to the philosophical understanding of God and his relations with man.

For such systems, reference to precedent and authorities was insufficient. Besides, it was found that the very axioms of tradition differed: for example, one of the Church fathers might contradict another. The spirit that sought a perfect order in society and a perfect order in the universe could not tolerate such ambiguities. In order to resolve them and to proceed beyond the frontiers established by the past, a new tool was needed. That tool was reason.

Today, when we take reason for granted and when, under the influence of Marx and Freud and the scientific method, we are often even suspicious of it, it is difficult to imagine the vernal enthusiasm of the philosophers in the twelfth and thirteenth centuries when they discovered this tool. To be sure, men had used reason ever since they became men, and the sophisticated use of reason in philosophical speculation was highly developed by the ancient Greeks. The fathers of the Church and earlier theologians were aware of Greek rational thought and had applied it to their early theological syntheses. But the excitement of those first efforts by Justin Martyr and of their fullest development by Augustine had long been submerged in exaggerated humility and respect for the past. The

173

ancient innovators had themselves become authorities. Now the scholastics broke the bonds of authority and with zest and excitement determined to apply reason systematically and in logical progression to every aspect of human knowledge. The analogy that springs to mind immediately is the scientific spirit of the nineteenth and twentieth centuries: vigorous, creative, heady, a bit arrogant, confident (until recently) of its ability to probe every dark corner of the universe and to answer all questions. The rational spirit of the twelfth and thirteenth centuries was enthusiastically applied not only to theology and philosophy, but to civil and canon law, to political theory, and to medicine and the other sciences.

The first of the great scholastics was St. Anselm (1033–1109), abbot of Bec and then, as archbishop of Canterbury, the opponent of William II and Henry I. As energetic in philosophy as in politics, Anselm wrote a number of theological works, the most important of which are the *Proslogium,* the *Monologium,* and the tract *Cur Deus Homo* ("Why God Became Man").

In the *Proslogium* Anselm expressed for the first time the ontological argument for the existence of God. Not a proof in the ordinary sense of the word, but a statement that the existence of God is self-evident, the ontological argument has been challenged and reaffirmed by philosophers from Anselm's time to our own. God is defined in such a way, Anselm implied, that he necessarily exists.

In the *Monologium,* Anselm proceeded to offer proofs for the existence of God based upon experience. The ontological argument is an a priori proof, of the Platonic and Augustinian variety, in which truth is achieved through introspection; the arguments of the *Monologium* are a posteriori, resting upon observation, and these look forward to the Aristotelian method used by Aquinas. The further significance of the *Monologium* is in its manner of proceeding step-by-step in logically consequent fashion. It is this thorough, rational, tightly knit, and logical procedure that caused Anselm to be named the "father of scholasticism."

Anselm taught and wrote at Bec, a monastic school, and another great theologian of the twelfth century was also a monk, the great Cistercian St. Bernard. More even than most great men, Bernard refuses to fit into any category: harsh, yet filled with love; an ascetic recluse, yet a friend of kings and wielder of great political influence; a mystic and prophet, yet devoted to the spirit of order. Bernard cannot be classified as a scholastic, but his approach to mysticism was logical and systematic.

The thrust of ecclesiastical order had brought about a riposte of the prophetic spirit in many forms, including mysticism, which from the twelfth through the seventeenth centuries enjoyed a currency throughout Christendom greater than either before or after. But mysticism itself was affected by the prevailing urge to intellectual order. In his *Steps of Humility,* St. Bernard developed mystical theology—the exposition in orderly, consequent fashion of the steps leading to, and away from, the mystical experience. A thirteenth-century example of mystical theology is St. Bonaventure's *The Mind's Road to God.* Both treatises contrast with the more personal mysticism of the twelfth-century school of St. Victor, and even more with the ecstatic, symbolic, and exalted writings of later mystics like John of the Cross, or even with Bernard's own poetry.

Bernard was a man of strong opinions and the chief opponent of another man who made great contributions to the development of scholasticism: Peter Abelard (1079–1142). Unlike the monastics Anselm and Bernard, Abelard had his base of operations in the schools of Paris, now emerging as centers of scholastic thought. Trained in dialectic and in theology, Abelard's brilliant and aggressive mind contributed greatly to the development of early scholasticism. He offered a solution to the heated debate over universals, arguing against realists that words or ideas had no independent existence of their own, and against the nominalists that ideas were not simply arbitrary, names but possessed a real and useful existence as concepts within the human mind.

Abelard's difficulties arose from the application of his keen logic to theological problems. In his famous *Sic et Non* ("Yes and No"), Abelard assembled a list of 158 theological propositions and then showed how in each of them could be found opinions of the Church fathers that were diametrically opposed to one another. The implications were clear: one could cite authorities for any theological position. Therefore, Abelard argued, the reason of the individual must be applied to the solution of theological problems. It was not Abelard's belief in reason in itself that was unusual. Under the spell of the Greek tradition, Christianity had always placed great stock in reason; and from the end of the eleventh century men like St. Anselm had replaced the older, rambling theological style with logical, orderly development of their arguments. This indeed was the essence of scholasticism. But Abelard's views seemed to St. Bernard and others to be extreme in their intellectualism. At a time when the humanity of Christ was being increasingly emphasized, Abelard appeared to consider him an abstraction, less the God-man who suffered for us on the Cross than a remote source of ethical teachings whose value could be proved, and whose details could be elicited, by the application of logic.

This excessive intellectualism was supplemented by an arrogant and rash personality that brought down upon Abelard not only corporal punishment for his affair with his pupil Héloïse, but ecclesiastical condemnation of many of his theological propositions as heretical. It is difficult today to determine what really was heretical about his doctrine, even by the standards of the narrower theologians of Abelard's day, except for a few passages in which he seems to exaggerate the role of free will in Pelagian fashion. There is no reason to doubt his claim in a letter to Héloïse that he at no time wished to deny any part of the orthodox faith; indeed, he believed that it was possible to convert heretics and infidels the more readily by the use of reason. It seems to have been less the content of his theology than his personal arrogance that earned him his censure. His strong defense of reason against tradition and his use of the method of opposing authorities and then resolving the opposition by the use of logic were of immense importance in shaping the course of later scholasticism.

The implications of Abelard's method were made most fully explicit by the greatest scholastic philosopher and theologian, Thomas Aquinas (1223–1274). This extraordinary man was destined by his wealthy parents to a high post in the hierarchy, but as a child he had already shown a tendency to scholarship instead of politics. He refused the offices that his father offered to procure for him and went instead to join the mendicant order of St. Dominic. Large and slow-moving, he was nicknamed the Dumb Ox by his teachers and fellow students until he demonstrated in debate that he was able to out-argue his professors. He studied and then taught at the University of Paris, where his piety and brilliance, as well as his noble connections, made him a frequent guest at the court of Louis IX. The author of many tracts on philosophy and political theory as well as of great theological *compendia,* he is said to have kept several secretaries busy at once with his dictation.

The two works that have earned him his reputation as the greatest systematic theologian in history are the *Summa Theologica,* a textbook for advanced students, and the *Summa Contra Gentiles* ("Summa against the Unbelievers"), which, being designed to convince Moslems, Jews, heretics, and the ignorant of the truth of the Christian faith, is a more elementary, and consequently a more fully explained, summary of Christian doctrine. In these works Aquinas at once perfected the scholastic method and incorporated into a new synthesis the recently rediscovered Greek thought. The supplanting of Platonic and Augustinian by Aristotelian thought is symbolized in the fact that Thomas commonly referred to Aristotle simply as "the Philosopher."

Thomas's method was to begin with the most fundamental questions of theology, and then to pursue each with all of its implications. The *Summae* are closely knit and organized with Euclidean precision. Following Abelard, Aquinas began each step of his demonstration by raising a question (for example, "Whether God exists?"). He then went on to state the philosophical objections to the existence of God (for example, "It seems that God does not exist; because if one of two contraries be infinite, the other would be altogether destroyed."). After stating, fully and as strongly as possible, all the objections, he then set forth one or more statements from the Bible or the fathers of the Church (for example, "On the contrary, it is said in the person of God: 'I am who am' [Exodus, 3:14]"). Finally, he went on to use his own reason to resolve the problem ("I answer that..."; in answer to the problem of God's existence, he propounded his famous five proofs based upon experience).

The scope of the *Summae* includes all that might be asked of God and God's ways with the world: the nature of truth and the way to obtain it, the nature of God, the attributes of God, the action of God in the world, the creation and the nature of the universe and its variety, the eternity of the universe and the nature of time, the problem of the existence and nature of evil, the nature of man, the spirit and the soul, moral good and evil, the immortality of the soul, the place of the angels and of Satan, free will, providence and predestination, salvation. These problems are studied in such complete detail that Thomas's system itself later became established as authoritative in Catholic thought. Certain Catholics continue to regard it as the clearest expression to date of absolute truth. Others would like to apply the method, if not the content, of Thomism to today's questions. Even those who no longer find Thomism convincing or useful cannot fail to be impressed by the intellectual beauty and grandeur of the system, so complete and clear is each part, so perfectly orchestrated are all the parts, and so internally balanced and consistent is the whole.

Even Aquinas had difficulty in making his views prevail during his own lifetime, and no sooner was scholasticism firmly established than it began to decline. The thought of Duns Scotus (c. 1270–

1308), a Franciscan and the most intricate of all the scholastics, is symptomatic of the causes of decline. So perfectly had Thomas raised and answered the basic questions, that his successors, like Duns, were obliged to turn to more and more obscure questions or to more and more complex solutions of old ones. Aquinas's proofs of the existence of God are relatively simple and easy to follow, but Duns's are so long and intricate as to be almost opaque to anyone not long-trained in scholastic expression. Duns's followers became even more obscure and unconvincing than their master, and the later Protestant Reformers came to call anyone teaching a tortuous and incomprehensible doctrine a "dunce," after the great Scot. On the other hand, Scotus was attracted by the mystical doctrine that human reason was incapable of finding out anything certain about God at all.

This kind of difficulty appeared even more clearly in the works of Siger of Brabant (c. 1240–1284) and William of Ockham (c. 1300–1349). Siger propounded the doctrine of the two truths, arguing that reason and revelation, though both true, are often mutually contradictory. When they are, it is futile to try to reconcile them. We must accept both truths, each in its compartment, and not try to synthesize them. Ockham argued, in similar fashion, that faith and reason, both necessary to man, could not be brought together. In part of his life man should follow faith, in part of his life he should follow reason; and he should not be dismayed at contradictions.

Thus at the very time that scholasticism seemed to have succeeded in producing a view of the world at once internally coherent and corresponding to objective reality, some of the most intelligent scholastics were questioning whether this was indeed possible. There is here, once again, an analogy to modern scientists, who now tend to say, unlike their predecessors of forty years ago, that they are incapable of finding truth and even uninterested in a search for truth that they know will be futile. They are satisfied when theories "work out," i.e., when they produce results, and they no longer claim to be able to establish objective reality.

Scholasticism continued through the fourteenth and fifteenth centuries; but, lacking conviction in its ability to find the truth, it degenerated more and more into games with words, and it lost the general assent of the community. In the realm of the intellect as well as in that of politics, the search for Christian order was vigorous and brilliant but not wholly successful. And in the intellectual as well as in the political sphere, the fourteenth and fifteenth centuries saw the triumph of prophecy over order.

XII Christianity in the Autumn of the Middle Ages

The years 1300 to 1500, like those from 250 to 700, are a transition period. Depending upon whether one is looking backwards or forwards, the era is either the "autumn of the Middle Ages" or the "Renaissance." All periods are periods of change, but these two centuries saw the beginning of a real departure from the principles of order that had long characterized medieval Christianity. The ideal of a unified Christian society was yielding to royal nationalism in northern Europe and to urban particularism in Italy; in the East, Greek Orthodox Christianity suffered almost total eclipse as a result of the conquest of the Byzantine Empire by the Turks, completed in 1453; the monarchy of the papacy in the Church was challenged from several sides; confidence was fading in the ability of reason to build an intellectual order corresponding to objective reality. The reactions generated by the temporary triumph of the spirit of order now gained greater strength as order waned.

Behind these shifts in attitude lay increasingly rapid changes in society as a whole. The growth in power of the towns and their merchants, on the one hand, and of the kings and their governments, on the other, encouraged a rising secularism. A series of

181

famines and plagues in the fourteenth and fifteenth centuries brought about a decline of population that created great dislocations of agricultural society and provoked peasants' revolts and uprisings. Owing to the emergence of more literate leaders and to the growth of a sense of common cause, the free peasants and the city laborers took a more active part both in politics and in the Church. In both Church and State was emerging the idea that the "people" (which usually still meant free men of a certain stature) had a right to be taken into account—partly because of the need of governments whose demands and scope were growing for a wider basis of support; partly because of the rise, for other practical reasons, of representative assemblies in both the cities and the kingdoms; and partly because of the development of political theories like those of Marsilius of Padua.

Marsilius upheld the ascending theory of sovereignty, arguing that God's authority is delegated to the "people" (i.e., the people of responsibility and social stature), who in turn choose their rulers. The rulers—princes or popes—are merely the "ruling part" *(pars principans)* of the community. They are responsible not only to God *for* the people, but to God *through* the people. They are public servants subject to dismissal, not rulers by divine election.

The papacy in these two centuries gradually lost its position at the center of Christian society. It was not that there were no good or able popes, or that there were no theoreticians to defend papal supremacy, but that the political, social, and intellectual climate offered other alternatives and that circumstances arose that made those alternatives seem plausible.

The first blow to the papacy was the kidnapping of Boniface

VIII in 1303, followed by the election of Clement V (1305–1314), who moved the papacy to Avignon and was a willing tool of the policies of King Philip IV. The popes remained at Avignon until 1377 in what was called the Babylonian Captivity, after the biblical episode of the Jews' enslavement by the Babylonians in the sixth century B.C. The decadence of the Avignon papacy has, however, been exaggerated until recently by historians. The Avignon popes continued to exercise the power of appointing bishops in wide areas of Europe. The papal administration continued to grow in complexity and power, and a pope like Benedict XII (1334–1342), who used his influence to effect a general reform of the religious orders, was not atypical either in his piety or in his energy. After Clement V, the Avignon popes were not minions of the French monarchy. There is little evidence that there was any widespread disaffection from the papacy simply because it was established at Avignon. Indeed, the arguments of Philip IV for the salutary effect of the removal of the pope from the intrigues of the Roman nobility had some validity.

The worst aspect of the Avignon papacy was in the difficulties it foreshadowed. These difficulties were partly owing to the fact that everyone knew that the papacy belonged at Rome and would eventually return there, so that the election of a Roman pope and a consequent schism was always a possibility, and partly the result of the growth in power of the papal administration itself, the curia. The cardinals who dominated the curia had long been accustomed to thinking of themselves as sharing with the pope the primacy of the *ecclesia romana.* In 1352, inspired by this tradition and perhaps also by the growing power of the kings' councils in the secular states, they issued a document demanding that in future conclaves a papal candidate must bind himself before his election to follow the policies recommended by the cardinals.

Events soon transformed these potential weaknesses into actuality. In 1377 Pope Gregory XI (1370–1378) elected to return to Rome in spite of unsettled conditions there, and in the next year he died. Amidst great confusion in a situation where the papal court had not yet really been transferred back to Rome, a group of cardinals in Rome hastily elected Pope Urban VI (1378–1389), a man of violent temper, who undertook to break the power of the cardinals long before he had the requisite support or influence. Accordingly, some of the cardinals met again and elected Clement VII (1378–1394), who chose to retain the papal seat at Avignon. From 1378 to 1409 there were two popes, one at Avignon and one at Rome, and there was no authority to judge which was legitimate. Kings supported one or the other according to policy: the king of France and his allies backed the Avignonese popes, and the king of England and his allies naturally supported the Romans.

The Great Schism had three important effects on ecclesiastical order. First it permitted the kings to reintroduce secular politics into the Church to a degree unknown since the early eleventh century. In France, the king and the civil lawyers of his *parlement* argued that the French Church was, except for due honor and reverence, independent of the papacy. They replaced papal with royal control over the election of bishops wherever possible, and they supported conciliar theories that would have weakened the papacy in favor of the bishops, whom the king might thus the more easily control. This ecclesiastical nationalism, called Gallicanism in France, was reflected to one degree or another in the politics of England, Germany, and practically every country of Europe.

The second effect was that respect for the papacy greatly declined among politicians, scholars, and the people at large. The spectacle of two popes excommunicating and doing political battle with each other could scarcely elicit the same kind of awe that Innocent III or even Boniface VIII could engender.

The third effect was the rise of conciliarism. The conciliar theory, stated in its simplest terms, is that the supreme authority in Christendom is not the pope, but a general council of bishops. The theory has its ultimate origins in the ancient idea of the collegiality of the bishops, of whom the pope is only *primus inter pares*— an idea that had always had a certain currency until the papal revolution of the eleventh century. At that time it was given impetus by certain polemicists, both anti-imperialists, who emphasized the dignity of the bishops, and imperialists, who wished to use the bishops as a curb to the power of the pope.

The kings of the fourteenth and fifteenth centuries found the idea of the collegiality of bishops attractive because it promised to limit papal interference in their countries; and it was reinforced by the ascending theories of government like those of Marsilius of Padua, who applied them in his writings directly to the Church as well as to the secular power. Ultimate authority under God rested with the Christian people, who delegated it to their representatives, the bishops. The bishops then chose a pope to whom they in turn delegated certain powers. The pope was responsible to the bishops, the bishops to the people, and the people to God. Conciliar theories were worked out in great detail and sophistication and with great attention paid to the canons and traditions of the past by a number of scholars, the most influential of whom was Jean Gerson (1364–1429), professor of theology and later chancellor at the University of Paris.

It was the practical need to resolve the Great Schism that enabled Gerson and his fellow scholars to transform theory into practice. It was evident that the theory that all disputes could be referred ultimately to the pope was not convincing when there were two antagonistic popes; and the conciliarists raised other spectral possibilities: suppose, there being only one pope, he should go mad or prove a monster of depravity? Under certain circumstances at least, another authority than the pope must be able to summon and preside over a council. By 1408 it appeared that the schism was going to be interminable, and most of the cardinals, both at Rome and at Avignon, agreed to hold a council to resolve it. This council met at Pisa in 1409 and decided to end the schism by declaring both claimants deposed and choosing a new pope, Alexander V (1409–1410). But the Roman pope, backed by the southern Italians, and the Avignonese pope, backed by the kings of Scotland and Aragon, refused to abide by the decisions of the council. There were now three vicars of Christ.

The situation, already intolerable, showed signs of growing worse: it seemed that the number of popes possible at one time was unlimited. With a sense of great urgency, the conciliarists pressed their doctrines and, with the aid of the Emperor Sigismund (1410–1437), induced the Pisan pope, John XXIII,[1] to call another general council. This, the sixteenth ecumenical council, assembled at Constance in 1414 and, in an effort to escape the intolerable pressures of the schism, passed the decree *Sacrosancta* (1415), which fulfilled the dearest wishes of the conciliarists. "The holy Council of Constance," said the decree, "declares...that it is a General Council...and that therefore it has its authority immediately from Christ; and that all men, of every rank and condition, including the Pope himself, is bound to obey it in matters concerning the Faith, the abolition of the schism, and the reformation of the Church of God in its head and its members."[2] The council went on in 1417 to depose all three claimants to the papacy and to appoint a pope, Martin V (1417–1431), who after further difficulties was at last generally recognized throughout Europe.

The triumph of the conciliarists was short-lived. At the Council of Ferrara-Florence, which met from 1438, the pope reasserted his power and domination; the decree *Frequens* of Constance calling for frequent general councils was ignored; and in 1460 Pius II in his bull *Execrabilis* declared that the notion that a council was superior to the pope was rebellious, poisonous, erroneous, and detestable.

The monarchy of the papacy over the Church continued to grow in the fifteenth and sixteenth centuries, but at the same time the general influence of the papacy in society was greatly diminished. Royalism and nationalism enjoyed successes more permanent than those of conciliarism; the papacy became again immersed in petty Italian politics; popular disaffection was widespread. The papacy's failure to regain either political or moral

---

[1] The modern papacy, by assigning the same title to John XXIII (1958–1963), implies that it accepts as valid only the Roman line of popes during the schism.

[2] Henry Bettenson, ed. and trans., *Documents of the Christian Church*, 2d ed. (London, 1963), p. 189.

leadership in society resulted ultimately in the Protestant Reformation of the sixteenth century.

Movements that had begun in reaction to the rise of ecclesiastical order now grew stronger with its decline. On the one hand secularism and indifference to religion spread. It is an absurdity to suppose that everyone in the earlier Middle Ages was pious and spiritual, but few cared overtly to deny or to scoff at the principles of religion. But from the eleventh and twelfth century, poets, many of them students or even ordained priests, produced quantities of light literature that was overtly worldly, ironically skeptical, or sometimes simply blasphemous—like the piece called "The Council of Remiremont," in which a group of nuns debate whether a layman or a priest makes a better lover. The ethic of courtly love, invented by the poets of the mid-eleventh century and for centuries taken up by the nobility with varying degrees of seriousness, was by almost any standards idolatrous in making the noble married lady an object of worship and adoration to her lover—who obeyed her, trembled in her presence, and in every way treated her as if she were God.

Some took these games less seriously than others, and neither the student songs nor the courtly love ethic represents a formal break with Christian orthodoxy. But they are representative of the growing secular spirit, which took quite serious and important forms in the later Middle Ages, in the wholly worldly politics of the princes and in the wholly worldly commercial interests of the merchants.

Diametrically opposed to secularism, yet like secularism encouraged by the decline of ecclesiastical order, was the advance of the prophetic spirit among both the clergy and the laity. As in the Protestant Reformation, the spirit of prophecy in the fourteenth and fifteenth centuries moved with particular vigor among the laity. Lay piety was already robust in the twelfth and thirteenth centuries, as we have seen; and its later strength is in part the result of a natural growth and in part one manifestation of the deep social dislocation brought about by the economic decline and by the terrible famines and plagues of the time.

Some popular piety, indeed, became very grotesque. The obsessive preoccupation with death is visible in its personification in art, and even more in the ghastly mementos of decay that appeared everywhere. It became common, for example, to decorate tombs with representations of the dead being eaten by worms or toads. A favorite device was to sculpt a tomb on two levels: on top, an effigy of the dead person clothed and recumbent in peace; underneath, often behind a grille, a representation of the same person rotting, or as a skeleton. What monstrosities were perpetuated at the less permanent graves of the simple people, we do not know; but we do know that alive they performed "dances of death" or, joined in flagellant societies, wandered about the countryside whipping one another. These perversions of the prophetic spirit have few precedents or imitations in the history of Christianity; rather than the natural outgrowth of anything in the medieval Church, they represent the attunement of religious expression to the fortunately temporary needs of a society obsessed with fear of plague and famine.

There were healthier manifestations of the prophetic spirit among the laity. In the Low Countries, for example, the mystical teachings of Jan van Ruysbroeck (1293–1381)and Gerard Groote (1340–1384) prompted the rise of a lay organization called the Brethren of the Common Life. These people lived a simple community life devoted to prayer, book-copying, and study of the Bible.

The spirit of prophecy brought forth among both clergy and laity new and powerful manifestations of Reformist dissent. It would be a mistake to suppose, as some Protestant historians have done in order to explain and justify the Protestant Reformation, that the Church of the fourteenth and fifteenth centuries was any more morally corrupt than at most other times in its history. Rather, the decline of ecclesiastical order rendered the Church authorities less vigorous in their efforts to combat corruption than they had been since the early eleventh century. As in the eleventh century, the result was impatience with the authorities—impatience that often drove people beyond the bounds of orthodoxy in their demands for reform. Because of increased literacy, increased popular participation in affairs, and greater social unrest, the dissent of the later Middle Ages attracted more support than had the earlier Reformist movements.

The two most important Reformists of the period were John Wyclif (c. 1320–1384) in England and John Hus (1369–1415) in Bohemia. Of the two, Hus was much more conservative; and though he was burned for heresy by the Council of Constance in 1415, some modern historians doubt that the charges were justified even by the criteria of the time.

Wyclif's doctrine was much more overtly revolutionary. A professor at Oxford, he attacked papal supremacy in the Church, denied transubstantiation, questioned that the Mass was the center of Christian worship, and eventually expressed doubts about the need of any kind of priesthood. Wyclif encouraged a translation of the Bible into English, with the idea that every Christian ought to read and interpret the Scriptures for himself. In 1382 he was condemned by a synod in London and ordered to remain in his own parish without preaching. Wyclif had attracted a number of followers at the university and among the gentry, and for a while after his death these followers, called Lollards (Dutch *lollaerd,* "babbler"), continued to wander about preaching from the vernacular Scriptures.

Wyclif and the Lollards, like previous Reformists, wished to teach the people to regain through individual meditation and reading of the Scriptures a direct personal experience of God. The Church of order, with its hierarchy, its priesthood, its sacraments, and its often unintelligible liturgy, seemed to the Lollards an impediment, rather than an aid, to grace. Though there is no direct connection between the Wycliffites, Hussites, and other late medieval Reformists and the Protestants of the Reformation, it is clear that in some areas, England and Bohemia for instance, the success of the Reformation was rendered easier by the fact that the populace was not wholly unfamiliar with these ideas.

The most profound expression of the prophetic spirit during the Middle Ages was mysticism. Generally speaking, mysticism has played a greater role in religions like Hinduism and Buddhism, where moral law and intellectual truth do not receive as much emphasis as they have in Christianity, or, for that matter, in Judaism or in Islam. Mysticism is a direct and personal encounter with God. As such, it is not encouraged by the spirit of political, moral, or intellectual order.

In Christianity, it is a fulfillment of the prophetic tradition. Christian mysticism derives its biblical justification from the withdrawal of Christ into the desert, and later into Gethsemane, to contemplate, and from the words of Christ to Mary, the sister of Martha, that she had chosen the better part by sitting quietly and hearing the word of God rather than running about doing good works. Mysticism is not the only kind of contemplation possible. The tradition of monastic withdrawal and contemplation in the first few centuries of the Church was not mystical. Rather, it was an effort to live a completely moral and worthy life by removing all worldly distractions. The aim of contemplation is the living of the perfect Christian life, and this goal was achieved by saints who were not necessarily mystics.

And yet the spirit of contemplation could not but encourage mysticism. St. Paul had urged that we empty ourselves out and bring in Christ instead, so that "I no longer live, but Christ lives in me." The systematic turning of the mind from the things of this world to contemplation of the world of God brings us nearer to the divine experience. Thus it was among those who practiced contemplation that mysticism arose.

Christian mysticism was encouraged by the writings of St. Augustine, who, though not wholly a mystic himself, was enough of one to understand it and intellectually brilliant enough to express it intelligibly. Augustine, following both Paul and Plato, believed that the phenomenal world was a less real reflection or projection of the world of ideas or the world of God. In order to attain to reality, then, one must penetrate the world of appearances to the real world. But there are two ways of doing this, both requiring meditation and contemplation. One is by means of the intellect: by first examining the world around us, and then our own minds, for analogies of God, we can penetrate behind appearances to some idea, however imperfect, of reality. In this way we get at truth, and the truth makes us understand not only the nature of the cosmos but the nature of the good, truly Christian life. The intellect can thus provide us with metaphysical and moral proof. But the religious spirit is not satisfied with *knowledge*; it wishes not so much to *know* as to *experience* God, and to unite the soul with him. To have this experience, it is necessary to seek God not with the intellect, but with love.

The sixth-century Syrian monk Pseudo-Dionysius the Areopagite and his followers, especially John Scotus Eriugena, did much for the development of mysticism with the negative theology they had derived from that of St. Augustine. They argued that God is so wholly above the categories of the human intellect that man can never know him. The way of the intellect, though not wholly futile, cannot lead us very far in our search for God.

As long as the practical dislocations and disorders of society demanded that the Church be a bulwark of social order, as long as the search for organization and structure in the Church was uppermost, mysticism was not encouraged. The domination of the Christian thought of the eleventh through thirteenth centuries by rational scholasticism, with its attempt to build a complete, orderly intellectual system of the world, did not encourage mysticism. But already, from the beginning of the twelfth century, the countercurrent was running, owing to the settling of society and the consequent freeing of the monasteries from many of their utilitarian functions.

The new orders, with their emphasis upon contemplation, like the Cistercians and Carthusians, or the Dominicans and Franciscans later, gave new life to the prophetic spirit. St. Bernard the Cistercian and St. Bonaventure the Franciscan were both mystics, though the prevailing scholastic manner of thought encouraged them to attempt to formulate intellectual descriptions of an experience essentially ineffable. The Franciscans, whose taste ran to experience rather than to the rational metaphysics of the Dominicans, were the leaders both of scientific and of mystical thought, and Francis himself had been one of the simplest and most direct of the mystics.

With the general decline of ecclesiastical and intellectual order in the fourteenth century, mysticism became for the first time a common expression of Christian thought. In England, France, Germany, Italy, and Spain, from the fourteenth through the sixteenth centuries there was a great flowering of the mystical spirit.

On the one hand the mystical spirit was taken up by the laity in movements of popular devotion like the Brethren of the Common Life, and this simple spirit of mysticism was best expressed in the *Imitation of Christ* by Thomas a Kempis (1379–1471), an Augustinian canon. This treatise, because of its simplicity and personal appeal, became one of the most popular spiritual guides ever written. "Above all goods and in all things, my soul," said Thomas in his *Imitation of Christ,* "thou shalt rest in our Lord always"; and his advice as to how to attain this rest in God is the more convincing because of his understanding of, and sympathy with, human frailties and temptations.

Another example of the manifestation of the mystical spirit to a simple member of the laity is the life of Margery Kempe in England (born c. 1275). The Lord said to her in her mind, she tells us, that "though I withdraw sometimes the feeling of grace from thee, fear not therefore, for I am a hidden God within thee, so that thou shouldst have no vainglory.... Wheresoever God is heaven is, and God is in thy soul and many an angel is about thy soul to keep it both night and day. For when thou goest to church, I go with thee; when thou goest to thy bed, I go with thee; and when thou goest out of town I go with thee. Daughter, there was never child so submissive to the father as I will be to thee to help thee and to keep thee. . . ."³

There was, beyond the simple mystical tradition represented by Margery Kempe and Thomas a Kempis, a deeper, though no more strongly felt, mysticism flourishing in the monasteries. Meister Eckhart in Germany (1260–1327), St. Catherine of Siena (1347–1380), and in England Walter Hilton (d. 1396) and the unknown author of the *Cloud of Unknowing* (written c. 1345–1386) are among the best-known mystics of the fourteenth century. The culmination of the mystical tradition was the work of St. John of the Cross in sixteenth-century Spain.

The *Cloud of Unknowing* expresses in vivid terms the nature of the mystical experience. God calls the Christian spirit to lose itself in him, and "how sluggish and slothful the soul that does not respond to the Lord's attraction and invitation."⁴ Men are called to God in different ways, but the man who is called to the contemplative life must seek to lose himself in God completely. In order to do this, he must begin by turning his attention away from this world of illusion. He must put a mist of forgetfulness between himself and the things of this world. He must forget all desires, for intellectual truth as well as for carnal things. "There is no exception whatever, whether you think of [the things of this world] as physical or spiritual beings, or of their states or actions, or of their goodness or badness."⁵ This mist of forgetfulness can only be achieved after long discipline consisting of prayer, meditation, and deliberate mortification of the desires of the flesh by means of fasting and other ascetic practices. Having achieved forgetfulness of this world, the contemplative turns his gaze to God. But he does not expect or desire to *know about* God. " 'How

³*The Book of Margery Kempe,* Early English Text Society Original Series 212, 1940, pp. 249–250, cited by David Knowles, *The English Mystical Tradition* (New York, 1961), p. 145.
⁴The *Cloud of Unknowing,* Clifton Wolters, ed. and trans. (Baltimore, 1961), p. 52.
⁵*Ibid.,* p. 59.

am I to think of God Himself, and what is He?' and I cannot answer you except to say 'I do not know.'"[6] Between man and God there is a cloud of unknowing that cannot be penetrated by the intellect. The only way whatever that man has of coming to God is through love. "With a devout and kindling love ... try to penetrate that darkness above you. Strike that thick cloud of unknowing with the sharp dart of longing love."[7]

And so God, who is himself Love, is reached only by love itself. And when a man has penetrated that cloud of unknowing and come to God, and has poured out himself and filled himself with God, then the word of Paul is fulfilled that he lives no longer, but Christ in him.

The burning arrow of love is the symbol of the prophetic spirit without which the life of the Church would have died. It was the burning spirit of unquenchable love that called the Church again and again back to the essential Christian experience, which is the encounter of the soul with God. The mystics, the monks, the heretics, the missionaries, the martyrs, all kept the Church warm with the warmth of their fire.

And yet, sadly, that same fire of life lit fires of death for others—for heretics, for Jews, for Moslems, and for other Christians. As the *Cloud* says: "Or, again, they experience a spurious warmth, engendered by the fiend, their spiritual enemy, through their pride, and materialism, and spiritual dabbling. And yet, maybe, they imagine it to be the fire of love, lighted and fanned by the grace and goodness of the Holy Spirit."[8]

And so the Church needed not only to pass through the refiner's fire of prophecy, but to be molded by the formative touch of the hand of order. For it was the spirit of order that restrained the excesses of enthusiasm and kept the Church in touch with the needs of society, so that society might find its life expressed in the Church. It was the spirit of order that, holding to the process of

[6]*Ibid.*
[7]*Ibid.*, p. 60.
[8]*Ibid.*, p. 106.

gradual development, kept the teachings and practices of the Christian community within the bounds of tradition.

The spirit of order and the spirit of prophecy, the conservative reformer and the progressive reformer, the orthodox and the heretic, the layman and the monk, the pious peasant and the theologian, together gave balance to the Christian religion. The differences, the tensions, even the hostility between them, produced a medieval Christianity that was neither so esoteric as to divorce itself from the needs of society nor so utilitarian as to forget the nature of the basic religious experience. Medieval Christianity had failings, like any other manifestation of the human spirit, but as a whole it was a most creative and impressive contribution to the history of religion and to the history of Western civilization.

Significant Popes to 1500

Clement I (90–99)
Julius I (337–352)
Leo I (440–461)
Gelasius I (492–496)
Gregory I (590–604)
Honorius I (625–638)
Martin I (649–655)
Gregory II (715–731)
Gregory III (731–741)
Zachary (741–752)
Stephen III (752–757)*
Hadrian I (772–795)
Leo III (795–816)
Nicholas I (858–867)
Hadrian II (867–872)
John VIII (872–882)
Formosus (891–896)
Sergius III (904–911)
John XII (955–964)
Sylvester II (999–1003)
Gregory VI (1045–1046)
Leo IX (1048–1054)
Stephen IX (1057–1058)
Nicholas II (1059–1061)

Alexander II (1061–1073)
Gregory VII (1073–1085)
Urban II (1088–1099)
Paschal II (1099–1118)
Gelasius II (1118–1119)
Calixtus II (1119–1124)
Innocent II (1130–1143)
Eugene III (1145–1153)
Hadrian IV (1154–1159)
Alexander III (1159–1181)
Innocent III (1198–1216)
Honorius III (1216–1227)
Gregory IX (1227–1241)
Innocent IV (1243–1254)
Gregory X (1271–1276)
Boniface VIII (1294–1303)
Clement V (1305–1314)
Benedict XII (1334–1342)
Urban VI (1378–1389)
John XXIII (1410–1415)**
Martin V (1417–1431)
Pius II (1458–1464)
Alexander VI (1492–1503)

*Sometimes called Stephen II.
**Now considered an antipope.

Selected Bibliography

All titles are paperback editions unless preceded by an asterisk.

The best general history of the Church, when it is completed, will probably be Jean Daniélou and Henri Marrou, eds., *Christian Centuries* (London: Darton, Longman, and Todd, 1964–). At present the best series, though itself not yet complete, is Augustin Fliche and Emile Martin, eds., *Histoire de l'Eglise* (Paris: Bloud and Gay, 1935–). See also the up-to-date bibliography of Owen Chadwick, *The History of the Church: A Select Bibliography,* 2d ed. (London: Historical Association, 1966).

i. Prophecy and Order

There are few such perennial questions of debate as the nature of religion or the nature of Christianity. These questions will certainly never be wholly resolved, yet the advance of scholarship in the history of religions, in theology, in anthropology, and in psychology has improved our understanding of them.

William James, in his *The Varieties of Religious Experience* (New York: Collier, 1961; originally published 1902), was one of the first psychologists to offer an interpretation of religious phenomena that was at once dispassionate and sympathetic. Arthur Darby Nock, *Conversion* (New York: Oxford University Press, 1961; originally published London: Oxford University Press, 1933) is a learned study, in the Jamesian tradition, of the experience of conversion in the lives of some of the great early Christians like Augustine and Justin Martyr. The religious experience has been described in a number of brilliant and sensitive accounts in the twentieth century. Among them are C. S. Lewis, *Surprised by Joy* (London: Fontana, 1959; originally published London: Bles, 1955), an exceptionally beautiful and serene account, particularly of the author's childhood and youth; Miguel de Unamuno, *The Agony of Christianity* (New York: Ungar, 1960), a penetrating account of the dilemmas of Christianity by a man who described himself as a "Catholic heretic" and who suffered greatly in the Spanish

Civil War; Simone Weil, *Waiting for God* (New York: Capricorn, 1959; originally published New York: Putnam, 1951), a personal and almost mystical spiritual autobiography of a young Jewish woman attracted by, yet resistant to, Christianity, whose commitment to human love led her to serve in Spanish hospitals during the Civil War; and Dietrich Bonhoeffer, *Letters and Papers from Prison* (originally published in 1954 as *Prisoner for God*) (New York: Macmillan, 1962), the thoughts of a Protestant minister martyred by the Nazis, whose ideas have had great influence on current theological thought of the "secular city" variety. Another man whose personal religious insight was unusually penetrating and intense was the nineteenth-century Søren Kierkegaard (*Attack upon Christendom* [Boston: Beacon, 1956; originally published Princeton, N.J.: Princeton University Press, 1944]), famous as a forerunner of modern existentialism and existential theology.

Work in history and anthropology has added greatly to our understanding of the religious experience. One of the most influential books of the interwar period was Rudolf Otto, *The Idea of the Holy* (New York: Oxford University Press, 1958; originally published London: Oxford University Press, 1931), an attempt to define religion in terms of the experience of the Wholly Other or the *mysterium tremendum.* Currently, Mircea Eliade, of the University of Chicago, has explored with enormous insight and learning the notion of the sacred in both archaic and historical societies. Among his books are *Cosmos and History* (New York: Harper, 1959); *The Sacred and the Profane* (New York: Harper, 1959); and *Patterns in Comparative Religion* (New York: World, 1958). An excellent account of the evolution of religious ideas in the ancient world is F. M. Cornford, *From Religion to Philosophy* (New York: Harper, 1957).

An extraordinary number of films with exceptional religious significance have appeared in the course of the last two decades, including Bernanos's *Diary of a Country Priest;* the films of Ingmar Bergman and of Satyajit Ray; *The Pawnbroker*; and *The Red Balloon.*

ii. Primitive Christianity

The best book on the religious customs of the Jews before the time of Christ is Roland de Vaux, *Ancient Israel (New York: McGraw-Hill, 1961); a good history of the early Jews is Theophile James Meek, *Hebrew Origins* (New York: Harper, 1960; originally published 1936). Among the numerous good short summaries of the Dead Sea

Scrolls and their significance is A. Dupont-Sommer, *The Essene Writings from Qumran* (New York: Meridian, 1962). On the Greek background of Christian thought see Edwin Hatch, *The Influence of Greek Ideas on Christianity* (New York: Harper, 1957; first published as *The Influence of Greek Ideas and Usages upon the Christian Church*, London: Williams and Norgate, 1890). The historiography of the question of Jesus was summarized by Albert Schweitzer in his *The Quest of the Historical Jesus* (New York: Macmillan, 1961; first published, in German, 1906), and James Robinson has explored some of the contemporary approaches in his *New Quest of the Historical Jesus* (London: SCM Press, 1959). At present there is no book that systematically reviews all of the varieties of historical interpretation of the problem of Jesus since the time of Schweitzer. Rudolf Bultmann has been one of the most influential Christologists of the last few decades, one of his major expository works being *Primitive Christianity in Its Contemporary Setting* (New York: Meridian, 1956). Bultmann and Karl Kundsin explain the methodology of biblical criticism that Bultmann did much to spread and that still is very influential in their volume *Form Criticism* (New York: Harper, 1962; originally published 1934).

By far the best narrative history of the early Church available in English is Jean Daniélou and Henri Marrou, *The Christian Centuries,* Vol. I, *The First Six Hundred Years* (London: Darton, Longman, and Todd, 1964). This book is at once lucid and comprehensive, and it incorporates the most important scholarly discoveries and interpretations to the time of its publication. John Henry Newman's book *An Essay on the Development of Christian Doctrine* (New York: Doubleday, 1960) was the first to spell out a comprehensive theory of the development of Christian doctrines and institutions and has had an enormous influence upon the writing of Church history, particularly among Catholics. Its brilliance, erudition, and vigorous arguments make it still a book that any serious student of Church history must know.

Studies of the apostles include Oscar Cullmann, *Peter* (New York: Meridian, 1958) and the excellent study *St. Paul,* by Arthur Darby Nock (New York: Harper, 1963). Gerhart Ladner, *The Idea of Reform* (Cambridge, Mass.: Harvard University Press, 1959) is a brilliant study of the origins of historical consciousness and the concept of progress among the Church fathers. Harry A. Wolfson, *The Philosophy of the Church Fathers* (Cambridge, Mass.: Harvard University Press, 1956) is a classic. A readable selection from the writings of the Church fathers is Herbert A. Musurillo, *The Fathers of the Primitive Church* (New York: Mentor-Omega, 1966).

iii. The Peace of the Church

A good survey of the history of the later Roman Empire is A. H. M. Jones, *The Decline of the Ancient World* (New York: Holt, 1966). The political problems of Christianity with the empire are discussed by T. M. Parker, *Christianity and the State in the Light of History* (London: A. and C. Black, 1955); and the religious confrontation of the two is explored by the essays in Arnaldo Momigliano, *The Conflict between Paganism and Christianity in the Fourth Century* (New York: Oxford University Press, 1963). The religious policies of Constantine have been vigorously discussed in a great number of books since the publication of the classic work by Jakob Burckhardt, *The Age of Constantine the Great* (New York: Doubleday, 1960; originally published 1949). Some of the better more recent studies are Hermann Dörries, *Constantine and Religious Liberty*, translated by Roland Bainton (New Haven, Conn.: Yale University Press, 1960) and A. H. M. Jones, *Constantine and the Conversion of Europe* (New York: Collier, 1962). J. G. Davies, *The Early Christian Church* (New York: Doubleday, 1967) is a lucid short account of the Church in this period. The phenomenon of Gnosticism, so important for the development of Christian thought, has been best described by Hans Jonas, *The Gnostic Religion* (Boston: Beacon, 1963; originally published 1958). A good account of monastic attitudes and contributions is Jean Décarreaux, *Monks and Civilization* (London: Allen & Unwin, 1964).

iv. The Mind of the Church, 300–700

Standard and useful volumes on early Christian culture include Charles Norris Cochrane, *Christianity and Classical Culture* (New York: Oxford University Press, 1957; first published Oxford, Eng.: Clarendon Press, 1940); E. K. Rand, *Founders of the Middle Ages* (New York: Dover, 1957; first published 1928); and Henry Osborn Taylor, *The Emergence of Christian Culture in the West* (New York: Harper, 1958; originally published as *The Classical Heritage of the Middle Ages,* New York: Macmillan, 1901). Perhaps the best available book on the subject is now M. L. W. Laistner, *Thought and Letters in Western Europe A.D. 500–900* (Ithaca, N.Y.: Cornell University

Press, 1957). A good study of the roots of medieval literature is C. S. Lewis, *The Allegory of Love* (New York: Oxford University Press, 1958; originally published Oxford, Eng.: Clarendon Press, 1936). By far the best translation of any work of medieval literature is Frederick Bliss Luquiens's of *The Song of Roland* (New York: Macmillan, 1960), an accurate, sympathetic, and vigorous job that makes *Roland,* as it should be, a pleasure to read. A good account of medieval iconography is Emile Mâle, *The Gothic Image* (New York: Harper, 1958; originally published as *Religious Art in France in the Thirteenth Century,* New York: Dutton, 1913). Monastic literature and learning is explored by Jean Leclercq in *The Love of Learning and the Desire for God* (New York: Mentor-Omega, 1961). Among the good books on St. Augustine is Frederik van der Meer, *Augustine the Bishop* (New York: Harper, 1961). In his *Augustine Synthesis* (New York: Harper, 1958), Erich Przywara does a fine job of presenting Augustine's thought in ordered sequence by means of selections excerpted from the saint's writings.

v. The Formation of the Medieval Order, 700–900

C. Delisle Burns, *The First Europe* (London: Allen & Unwin, 1948) is a good account of the transition period of the early Middle Ages, though perhaps the most illuminating study is that of Wilhelm Levison, *England and the Continent in the Eighth Century* (New York: Oxford University Press, 1946). A great amount of illustrative matter is offered by Eleanor Shipley Duckett in her *Gateway to the Middle Ages,* Vol. I, *Italy;* Vol. II, *France and Britain;* Vol. III, *Monasticism* (Ann Arbor, Mich.: University of Michigan Press, 1961; originally published New York: Macmillan, 1938), and in her *The Wandering Saints of the Early Middle Ages* (New York: Norton, 1959). Excellent short accounts of Byzantium and Islam are Joan Hussey, *The Byzantine World* (New York: Harper, 1961; first published London: Hutchinson University Library, 1957); Bernard Lewis, *The Arabs in History* (New York: Harper, 1960; first published London: Hutchinson University Library, 1954); and Tor Andrae, *Mohammed: The Man and His Faith* (New York: Harper, 1960; first published New York: Barnes & Noble, 1957). The best account of the rise of the papacy is the thorough one by Walter Ullmann, *Growth of Papal Government in the Middle Ages,* 2d ed. (London: Methuen, 1962).

vi. Christianity in Society, 700–1050

This is a problem on which there is little literature in English, the best thorough account being that of Emile Amann and Auguste Dumas, *L'Eglise au pouvoir des laïques* (Paris: Bloud and Gay, 1948), a volume in the series by Augustin Fliche and Emile Martin, *Histoire de l'Eglise.* A good survey account of the whole period is that of Christopher Brooke, **Europe in the Central Middle Ages* (New York: Holt, 1964). Henry Charles Lea explored one aspect of sacerdotal morality in his **A History of Sacerdotal Celibacy in the Middle Ages,* 3d ed. (New York: Russell & Russell, 1957). A little-known but very useful illustrative monograph dealing with the temporal concerns of the bishops in the period is Edgar N. Johnson, **The Secular Activities of the German Episcopate* (Lincoln, Neb.: University of Nebraska Press, 1932).

vii. Reform *and* viii. Revolution

The movements of reform in the Church culminating in the papal revolution of the eleventh century have been studied from many different points of view. Schafer Williams has collected a good series of essays representative of different approaches in his pamphlet *The Gregorian Epoch: Reformation, Revolution, Reaction?* (New York: Heath, 1964). Gerd Tellenbach, **Church, State, and Christian Society at the Time of the Investiture Contest* (Oxford, Eng.: Blackwell, 1940) is an excellent discussion of the theories of papalists, imperialists, and monks. Norman F. Cantor describes the course of the papal revolution in England in his **Church, Kingship, and Lay Investiture in England 1089–1135* (Princeton, N.J.: Princeton University Press, 1958); and Cantor has written a very perceptive article on the radical changes in monasticism in the period: "The Crisis of Western Monasticism 1050–1130," *American Historical Review,* LXVI (1960). A broader view of English relations with the papacy, encompassing the Middle Ages as a whole, is that of Zachary N. Brooke, **The English Church and the Papacy,* 2d ed. (Cambridge, Eng.: Cambridge University Press, 1952). Jeffrey B. Russell, **Dissent and Reform in the Early Middle Ages* (Berkeley and Los Angeles: University of California Press, 1965) demonstrates the connection between the reform movements and movements of religious dissent. A group of readings with useful and learned comment is Brian Tierney, *The Crisis of Church and State 1050–1300* (Englewood Cliffs, N.J.: Prentice-Hall, 1964).

ix. The Riposte of the Prophetic Spirit

In former ages the literature of monasticism used to suffer from the defects of excessive piety, but this can hardly be said of the critical historical works of modern writers. The work of Dom David Knowles on English monasticism is monumental not only in scope but in scholarly excellence: *The Monastic Order in England,* 2d ed. (Cambridge, Eng.: Cambridge University Press, 1963); *The Religious Orders in England,* 3 vols. (Cambridge, Eng.: Cambridge University Press, 1948–59). Etienne Gilson, *The Mystical Theology of Saint Bernard* (New York: Sheed & Ward, 1940) is a study of the Cistercian's theology by one of the greatest modern historians of philosophy. Louis Bouyer, *The Cistercian Heritage* (Glen Rock, N.J.: Newman, 1958); Bede Jarrett, *The Life of Saint Dominic* (New York: Doubleday, 1964); and Paul Sabatier, *Life of Saint Francis of Assisi* (New York: Scribner, 1923) are other reputable works on medieval monasticism in the twelfth and thirteenth centuries. Among the better books on medieval mysticism are David Knowles, *The English Mystical Tradition* (New York: Harper, 1965; first published London: Burns and Oates, 1961) and two studies by Evelyn Underhill: *Mysticism* (New York: Dutton, 1961; first published 1930) and *The Essentials of Mysticism* (New York: Dutton, 1960). A good survey of the Catharists or Albigensians, though it is inaccurate in places, is Steven Runciman, *The Medieval Manichee* (New York: Compass, 1961; first published Cambridge, Eng.: Cambridge University Press, 1947).

x. The Offensive of the Papacy

Walter Ullmann, *Growth of Papal Government in the Middle Ages,* 2d ed. (London: Methuen, 1962) is very useful for the later period of medieval papal history as well as for the earlier; Ullmann's earlier book *Medieval Papalism* (London: Methuen, 1949) is a discussion of the papal theories of the later Middle Ages. A good recent collection dealing with the papacy's relations with England is Clifford H. Lawrence, ed., *The English Church and the Papacy in the Middle Ages* (New York: Fordham University Press, 1965); and Charles T. Wood has edited a pamphlet containing selections dealing with the struggle between the papacy and France: *Philip the Fair and Boniface VIII* (New York: Holt, 1967). The best general account of the development of canon law is Robert C. Mortimer, *Western Canon Law* (Berkeley: University of California Press, 1953). On the Crusades, there are a number of excellent books. The most massive scholarly work, when completed, wil! be Kenneth M. Setton, ed., *A History of the Crusades,* 5 vols. projected (Philadelphia: University of Pennsylvania Press, 1955—). Steven Runciman, *A History of the Crusades,* 3 vols. (New York: Harper, 1964–67; first published Cambridge, Eng.: Cambridge University Press, 1951–55) is a colorful and accurate chronological account. A good interpretive book is Aziz S. Atiya, *Crusade, Commerce, and Culture* (New York: Wiley, 1962). The papacy's confrontation with dissent was the subject for Henry Charles Lea, *A History of the Inquisition of the Middle Ages,* 3 vols. (originally published 1888) (New York: Russell & Russell, 1956), one of the great monuments of medieval history and still extremely useful as a source of information. A recent account of the inquisition, and of heresy after 1250, is Gordon Leff, *Heresy in the Later Middle Ages* (Manchester, Eng.: Manchester University Press, 1967). A general account of medieval heresies is being prepared by Malcolm Lambert; and Walter Wakefield will soon publish a book of translations of many of the most important documents of medieval heresy. The confrontation of medieval Catholicism with Judaism is discussed by Joshua Trachtenberg, *The Devil and the Jews: the Medieval Conception of the Jew and Its Relation to Modern Antisemitism* (New York: Harper, 1966). Gavin Langmuir and Allan Cutler are preparing works on medieval anti-Semitism. Edward A. Synan comments on the sources in *The Popes and the Jews in the Middle Ages* (New York: Macmillan, 1965).

xi. The Scholastic Order, 1050–1300

There are more good books available in English on medieval philosophy than on any other aspect of medieval Christianity. Among general histories of medieval thought are: Frederick C. Copleston, *A History of Philosophy,* 2d ed., Vols. II and III (Garden City, N.Y.: Doubleday, 1961–63); David Knowles, *The Evolution of Medieval Thought* (Baltimore: Pelican, 1962); Gordon Leff, *Medieval Thought —Saint Augustine to Ockham* (Baltimore: Pelican, 1958); Julius R. Weinberg, *A Short History of Medieval Philosophy* (Princeton, N.J.: Princeton University Press, 1964); Etienne Gilson, *A History of Christian Philosophy* (New York: Random House, 1955). Josef Pieper, *Scholasticism* (New York: McGraw-Hill, 1960) is a good introduction to the kind of philosophy that dominated the twelfth and thirteenth centuries.

R. W. Southern, *Saint Anselm and His Biographer* (Cambridge,

Eng.: Cambridge University Press, 1963) is an excellent study of the ways of thought of the twelfth century, as could be expected from the author of *The Making of the Middle Ages* (New Haven, Conn.: Yale University Press, 1956), perhaps the finest introduction in English to medieval ways of thinking in general. Another brilliant book on medieval thought is R. R. Bolgar, *The Classical Heritage and Its Beneficiaries: From the Carolingian Age to the End of the Renaissance* (New York: Harper, 1964), which explores not only the evolution of medieval thought itself but the changing forms of society that helped to produce changes in intellectual expression. The clearest introduction to Aquinas is that of Frederick C. Copleston, *Aquinas* (Baltimore: Penguin, 1955); Etienne Gilson, *Heloise and Abelard* (Chicago: University of Chicago Press, 1951) is a good introduction to the career of the twelfth century's most notorious intellectual. Arthur O. Lovejoy, *The Great Chain of Being* (New York: Harper, 1960; originally published Cambridge, Mass.: Harvard University Press, 1936), a study of the assumptions of medieval men about order in the cosmos and in society, was the model for a whole generation of intellectual historians.

The standard work on medieval universities has long been J. H. Rashdall, *The Universities of Europe in the Middle Ages,* ed. M. Powicke and A. B. Emden, 3 vols. (Oxford, Eng.: Oxford University Press, 1936); a brief and lively account is that of Charles Homer Haskins, *The Rise of Universities* (Ithaca, N.Y.: Cornell University Press, 1957). On Jewish philosophy see Isaac Husik, *A History of Medieval Jewish Philosophy* (New York: Meridian, 1958); and on Islamic thought see Gustave von Grunebaum, *Medieval Islam,* 2d ed. (Chicago: University of Chicago Press, 1955).

xii. Christianity in the Autumn of the Middle Ages

A good general survey of later medieval history is Denys Hay, *Europe in the Fourteenth and Fifteenth Centuries* (New York: Holt, 1966). Brian Tierney, *Foundations of the Conciliar Theory* (Cambridge, Eng.: Cambridge University Press, 1955); Walter Ullmann, *The Origins of the Great Schism* (London: Burns, Oates, and Washbourne, 1948); and Ernest F. Jacob, *Essays in the Conciliar Epoch,* 3d ed. (Notre Dame, Ind.: University of Notre Dame Press, 1963) are among the best books on the decline of the medieval papacy, as is Guillaume Mollat, *The Popes at Avignon* (New York: Harper, 1965). K. B. McFarlane, *The Origins of Religious Dissent in*

England (New York: Collier, 1966; originally published as *John Wycliffe and the Beginnings of English Nonconformity* [London: English Universities Press, 1952]) is a good book on John Wyclif and his influence. See also Herbert B. Workman, *John Wyclif: a Study of the English Medieval Church* (Hamden: Archon Press, 1966). The difficult problem of witchcraft has been studied intelligently in recent years in a light but critical book by Elliot Rose, *A Razor for a Goat* (Toronto: University of Toronto Press, 1962), and by H. R. Trevor-Roper, "Witches and Witchcraft," *Encounter,* XXVIII (May and June, 1967). Another work on St. Francis has recently appeared in a good new edition: Omer Engelbert, *Saint Francis of Assisi: A Biography,* 2d ed., new translation by Eve Marie Cooper, revised and augmented by Ignatius Brady, O.F.M., and Raphael Brown (Chicago: Franciscan Herald Press, 1965). A good new book has just appeared on John Hus and the impact of his ideas on society: Howard Kaminsky, *A History of the Hussite Revolution* (Berkeley and Los Angeles: University of California Press, 1967). Matthew Spinka explores an aspect of Hussite theology in *John Hus' Concept of the Church* (Princeton, N.J.: Princeton University Press, 1966).

Index

207